Highs, Lows and Hypos
The Danny Sculthorpe Story

Danny Sculthorpe

and

Mike Appleton

Vertical Editions
www.verticaleditions.com

First published in the United Kingdom in 2017 by Vertical Editions, Unit 4a, Snaygill Industrial Estate, Skipton, North Yorkshire BD23 2QR

www.verticaleditions.com

ISBN 978-1-908847-07-2

A CIP catalogue record for this book is available from the British Library

Cover design by HBA, York

Printed and bound by Jellyfish Print Solutions, Swanmore, Hants

For my wife, Natalie, and children Ellie, Louie and Isla.
You are my rocks.

Contents

Acknowledgements

Danny and Mike would like to thank all the people who have helped to put this book together. In no particular order they are:

Karl Waddicor and all the team at Vertical Editions, Daniel Spencer, Bernard Platt, Ste Jones, Gareth Walker, Roy Garbett, Lee Robinson, Phil Wilkinson, Ryan Bradley, Tim Fisher, Michelle Cooper, Alice Stoker, Gary Miller, Iain MacCorquodale, Stuart Raper, Dr. Phil Cooper MBE, Tracey Haughton, Brian Carney, Steve Gill, Shayne McMenemy, Malcolm Rae OBE, Brian Carney, Dave Lyon, Terry Matterson, Colin Bland, Dave Williams, George Unsworth, Danny Nutley, Nathan Brown, Doug and Linda Sculthorpe, Emma Rosewarne, Martin Hall, Steve Bithell, Maurice Lindsay, Lee Sculthorpe, Kevin Sinfield MBE and Paul Sculthorpe MBE.

Mike would like to add personal thanks to Danny for letting him into the innermost and sensitive details of his life. Danny was the perfect subject, not afraid to answer tough questions and it can't have been easy for him to relate some of the stories. Mike feels privileged that Danny allowed him to pen his words and become an inspirational close friend in the process.

Foreword

Men compete with other men to know where they stand in the world and this helps them work out who they are.

This statement could not be truer of many of the rugby league players I have encountered. I first met with Danny Sculthorpe on a day when this measure had failed him; he had lost an answer to a question about his identity, an answer that such a huge part of his life up to that point, competition with other men, could no longer provide.

His world was confined to a sole seat; he was physically broken and unable to move due to pain that exceeded any scale my well-meaning enquiry offered. The question of who would beat who on Friday night or whether you saw the game last week were insignificant. Danny had spent the preceding days debating exactly how he could end his misery and lighten the load of his wife and family. He was torn and confused by his moral beliefs, his love for those who he would leave behind and an unusual emotion to Danny – fear.

Here is a man who had stories of a sporting career in one of the greatest games on the planet. His CV reads like a who's who of rugby league and he has played at the highest level for top clubs over a lengthy career as well as representing his country. For the sports fan, Danny's story will offer insight into the tough world of professional rugby and what it takes to be the best.

The questions that Danny brought to our meeting I was unable to answer. Who is Danny Sculthorpe? What was the point of his existence? The best I could do was to offer to stand by his side if he accepted my challenge to consider the response to his own enquiry.

This is where my attempt to write a foreword to a book that charts this man's journey falls short. Perhaps others should describe who he is as a husband, father, son and brother or tell you of the guy that now gives so freely of his own pain to help others. Danny speaks eloquently today about his personal journey; he tells his truth with the purpose of helping others to speak theirs and in doing so, I have no doubt that that Danny Sculthorpe changes and saves lives. He offers his time to **State of Mind**, an excellent organisation encouraging people to look after their mental health and he has spoken for our charity, **Sporting Chance**, in the hope that players, either in rugby league or across other sports, can address their problems in the same way Danny has himself.

There is an old tribal song that was sung on returning from battle. One of the lines translates as: 'To hear this song is the victory!'

So here is to the victor – Danny Sculthorpe, a man with a purpose.

Colin Bland
CEO, Sporting Chance, 2017

1

No Way Back

The engine was off, the lights killed and I stared blankly through the windscreen. All ahead of me was darkness. Outside was quiet. I sat motionless, lost in my own world, a painful, miserable reality that had consumed me for far too long. On my left was a bottle of gin, a four pack of beer and enough painkillers to do the job right. They were the most powerful the doctors could prescribe and in a short while I would feel nothing at all. How had it got to this? Why was I in this state? I'd had injuries before. Being hurt and playing hurt is part and parcel of being a professional rugby league player, but this pain was different. It was real.

My first injury was as an Under 13 taking part in a wheelbarrow race at the Waterhead Rugby Club in Oldham. My brother Paul had hold of my legs and was running as fast as he could. But I couldn't go as quickly as he could and he ended up kneeing me in the balls. One of my testicles went right up into my groin so I had to have it cut out and sewn back in.

I dislocated my kneecap playing for Royton Tigers, an injury that would eventually bring on my diabetes. They couldn't get it back in at the ground, but on the way to A and E the vibrations of the road knocked it back into its rightful place. It went again towards the back end of my career at Rochdale, but there was no easy fix, no road to bounce along and it had to be operated on.

I broke my ribs at Rochdale Hornets, damaged rib cartilage at Wigan and also had a sternum problem after I dropped a bar on myself when lifting weights. A prolapsed disc followed at the Warriors, which needed a discectomy and a laminectomy, and then the stitches burst, leaving me with internal bleeding and facing about three operations in four hours. I also had a piece of my jaw snapped after a botched dental procedure.

At Castleford I tried to give it to Wigan after they had released me and in a tackle I broke and dislocated my thumb on Bryn Hargreaves' head. Later in the year I tore my rotator cuff in the 'Battle of Belle Vue' against Wakefield as forward Adam Watene came in and gave me a good smash in a tackle. Relegation and another operation followed – one of three in total I'd have on my shoulders during my career. Playing for Wakefield, my thumb needed fixing again and I also broke my hand and needed a carpel tunnel operation. The bone didn't mend properly so that needed an operation, too.

And in my final season at the Wildcats I tore ankle ligaments on our pre-season training camp and that resulted in me being sent home and missing a fair chunk of the early part of the year.

Then came the serious ones that ended my playing days. I prolapsed a disc in training at Bradford and caught a massive infection that nearly killed me. I was in and out of hospital, had a spinal fusion, a disc taken out, part of my spine removed and two Hickman lines – silicone rubber tubes through which medication is administered – fitted through my chest to my heart. As I recovered, they had to cut away at my chest to take them out because the skin had grown around them – all done while I was awake.

After six months the Bulls tore up my contract without even coming to see me or bothering to get in contact. Then, after a hellish recovery, in what turned out to be my final game for Widnes, I got cannonball-tackled, which left me needing 22 operations on my right knee. *Twenty-two* surgeries, alongside the back problems, that have left me with foot drop and various other walking problems.

Add to this pulled calves, hamstrings, shin splints, cuts, bruises, clean-outs, playing with injections following a sternum injury, taking to the field the day before rotator cuff surgery and a long-term addiction to sleeping tablets and painkillers, it's fair to say I've had my gutful of injuries. I have various bits of metal in all parts of me and no doubt as I get older the stresses and strains of my career will lead to more severe arthritis and other problems. I already know I need more rotator cuff surgery.

But these are mere trivialities compared with depression.

It's thought that about one in 10 people have mixed anxiety and depression in the UK and I was part of those statistics. Depression consumed my every thought. Things got so bad after the Bulls tore up my contract that I started to contemplate ending my life. I couldn't do anything for myself and I couldn't earn for my young family. Not being here seemed the best option for all. I'd gone from being a well-paid professional athlete with a good career and good standing in the game to nothing, a nobody. I was an ex-player sat in the Jobcentre in Wigan hoping I could scrape enough money together to keep a roof over my family.

I'd be driving my car on the motorway to one of my

many hospital appointments and my mind would drift. The world would become a fuzzy, blurry place and I would get visions that would offer real clarity. I began to picture steering my car off the road into a wall or a bridge or somehow causing a big accident. Those images were all I could think about. I thought my kids and wife could do without me. Without Danny in their lives they could get on and not have a burden on their hands. Every day began with, 'Should I get in my car now and wrap it around a tree or maybe I should take all the tablets that are in the house?' It got to the point where those thoughts consumed me every second, of every minute, of every hour of the day.

Because of the back surgeries and subsequent infections, I was prescribed the most powerful painkillers you could get. They were much stronger than morphine and I had loads of the pills. I would neck them straight from the bottle on my worst days, but my body had become almost immune to the painkilling effect. Overdosing and taking my life would have been easy and I had been rehearsing the scenarios in my head.

Then one day I decided it was time. I found myself sitting in my car at Beacon Park in Wigan with the sole intention of ending my life. There were a few cars around me, but I was oblivious of them. At my side was a big box of tablets, a litre bottle of gin and several cans of beer and I was going to take the lot. I lifted the lid off the box and I stared at my fate. There were enough tablets there to have killed ten men and I was going to down the lot. I must have sat there for hours working myself up to do the deed; the same thought going through my mind that the world would be a better place without me.

Then a few hours later I found myself driving back home

to Wigan. I didn't have a clue what I was doing any more, but I must have made the subconscious decision to close the lid, turn on the engine and head home. To this day I don't remember putting the tablets and booze in my car, but it was pretty clear I had put them there – and just as clear as to what my plan was. My kids must have been at school and my wife, Natalie, out shopping. To this day I don't remember driving to Beacon Park or the drive home, only sitting in the car park, then arriving home and putting the tablets away before I tried to slot myself back into a normal life. Or as normal as I had made it; sitting on the sofa, lost in my own zone and not interacting with anyone. My life was confined to a single seat on a settee.

For a couple of days after I was angry and frustrated at myself that I hadn't gone through with it. I'd had a plan, a conclusion to work towards and now I was in no-man's-land because I hadn't seen it through. I felt ashamed with myself that I hadn't had the courage and conviction to take my own life.

I don't know what stopped me from going ahead with it. Perhaps in a split-second of clarity there was the one rational flicker of a thought about what I would leave behind and the devastation it would cause. There would be no way back and no second chances. Nat would be a widow, Louie and Ellie would no longer have had a father and Isla would never have been born. Mum and Dad would have lost their son and Paul and Lee a brother.

Mum, Dad and Nat had seen me spiralling lower and jointly decided that enough was enough. They had asked many times during the previous weeks if I was okay, but I'd always managed to avoid the issue by changing the subject or giving a curt answer of 'I'm fine'. But after the car park incident – of which they knew nothing at that time – I was at my lowest ebb and they had no intentions of being side-tracked or put off. They sat me down in the kitchen and insisted on getting some answers. And this time it all came out.

I explained everything. I sobbed and cried and told them how I was a failure, how I'd let them all down and how it would be better for them if I was dead. I described the thoughts and mental trauma going through my brain and told them how I'd contemplated taking my own life.

And that was the point at which I started to get better.

***

Is suicide selfish? I've listened to people and read many reports debating this question and I can answer it only from my own perspective. At my low point I was thinking that everyone would be better off without me and, as a result, their lives would improve. When I was contemplating suicide, I was making the argument in my head that I was thinking of the people close to me and how their lives would be better without me around and being a burden. I'd done thinking about having a future because I was consumed in my own mental pain and just wanted an escape. The problem was I was so consumed in my own misery that my thoughts were becoming twisted and I was using the argument of making my loved ones' lives better by taking mine as an excuse.

I had done the typical 'man' thing all my life. I was a rugby league player and a bloke who liked a laugh. I was a big drinker, too. I didn't know how to tell my wife that I was struggling with my mental health. I was a big, hard rugby player who was programmed not to show emotion or betray being hurt on the field. If I had, the opposition would have exploited me in the same way I would have done if it was the other way round.

But around that table with my family it at last all poured out. I had gone from being a successful professional sportsman to being nothing and it was all because of an injury that was no fault of my own. The subsequent back surgeries had left me in pain, I was on the dole and I was addicted to painkillers and doing 'cold turkey' trying to get off them. I had made a comeback at Widnes after working fucking hard off the field, but I was still using the painkillers which were on WADA's banned list and I was told I couldn't play until I stopped taking them. That was the final straw. My mental illness had stripped me of everything I enjoyed in the world and now I couldn't even play rugby, the only thing I knew, which meant I couldn't earn any money for my family.

My brain was scrambled and my personality had completely changed. I was no longer Danny the guy who liked to have a laugh and take the piss. I'd always been a confident lad, but all that had drained from me. I had no motivation to get up and do anything. I had two young kids, but they were a blur around me; echoes in the house. The sound was muffled and life was just passing me by.

I had always been an emotional guy; a real soft arse. If someone upset me, I would either cry or thump them. On the field I could use that emotion as anger. But even those raw emotions had drifted away from me. I was depressed, consumed in my own misery and lack of self-worth, and I had a sickly feeling in my stomach all the time.

I think depression is one of the worst things you can suffer from. It is a horrible illness because it is inside your head and no-one can see it. If you have a broken leg, then it is visible and you can get it fixed. If your head's not right, then it's totally different. There is nothing obvious to see and social stigma forces you to keep quiet. And if you're a sportsman, it is dangerous to speak out.

Thankfully that day in the kitchen I found the strength to talk to my family and it was the start of a long road. It's a journey I am still on in my work with State of Mind as I progress towards being a counsellor. One initial conversation, then hours and hours of talking, crying and repeating my thoughts have brought me back from the brink. It has been a most amazing process as I have progressively got everything off my chest and a massive weight has been lifted from my shoulders. But it hasn't just been me dealing with the depression; it has been through the efforts of my family and me fighting it together with the therapists who have helped and guided us, united as a team.

I realise I am lucky to have such a good, close-knit family. I had shut them out of my life for too long, but they are far too stubborn not to get to the bottom of what was going on. They had realised that things had gone really bad and that they needed to get me to open up and talk. Thankfully that evening in the kitchen they wouldn't allow me to fob them off and thankfully I was able to tell them everything.

In that car park I very nearly ended it all. I had enough tablets to kill a horse with alcohol to aid the process.

Fortunately something sparked in my mind and I decided not to go through with it.

This is the story of how I came back to life.

2

Rugby, Rugby, Rugby

I'd just scored a perfectly legitimate try when out of nowhere my brother Paul smashed me in the face. Needless to say I was indignant about it so aimed a right at him and next thing I knew we were rolling about on the floor, arms and legs flailing and fists landing on faces. It was a fairly typical Sunday afternoon scene at our house while Mum and Dad were at Oldham Cricket Club enjoying a few drinks.

I was six-years-old, Paul eight, and every Sunday would start off with a simple game of rugby on our knees using Dad's old rugby socks as a ball. And as usual Paul and I would end up scrapping. Our older brother Lee would let things go for a bit until it would need stopping before someone got seriously hurt. Weekend after weekend and month after month until one time it got serious.

I'd scored again and that resulted in the usual punches raining down on me. Lee had once again stepped in to pull us apart, but accidentally threw Paul through the TV cabinet which was in the corner of our big living room. We were all rough, tough lads, but waiting for Mum and Dad to come back and see the damage undermined our confidence. Once we had broken that cabinet we weren't as hard any more; nor were we DIY experts who could fix a broken screen and splintered wood.

As the youngest I would often get picked on by my brothers and it's fair to say with Paul in particular I had a frosty relationship. It must have been a pain for Paul when I was born because he wasn't the youngest any more. Mum and Dad wanted a girl, but gave up after me, clearly saving the best to last. Paul and I hated each other. We were phenomenally competitive, but never saw eye-to-eye and we each gave the other as good as we got.

On one occasion playing our living room rugby, I ducked one of his punches only to see him hit the wall flush on and break a knuckle. Another time after school I was at Glo and Fred's, my childminders, and Paul and Lee forgot to pick me up. They were due to collect me at 5.00pm but I was still waiting at 8.45. In fact, they remembered they were supposed to collect me only when Mum and Dad came home. As it turned out it wasn't too bad. There were other kids at the house to play with and have a good laugh. If I'd been at home we would probably have been fighting, so it was no bad thing to have a night off from that once in a while.

When we were kids, Paul and I knew what buttons to press to wind each other up. He would call me 'Fat Jabba' – I had a problem with my weight – and I would call him 'Skinny Gizzard' because he was stick-thin. As I got older, I got more sensitive about being overweight and Paul would take full advantage. He could see a weakness, the sibling rivalry would take over and the insults would fly in. I tried to blank it all out, but it would get to me. I would try to distract from it and show my Dad my side muscles – in reality they were rolls of fat!

It took until I was at former Warrington player Jon

Roper's wedding for Paul and me to make amends with both of us admitting to being a complete pain in the arse for all those years. I broke down and told him what I thought of him and apologised for being a nuisance. It wasn't jealousy or anything like that, I just never liked him when we were growing up and the feeling from Paul was likewise. I told him in floods of tears how much I looked up to him and we have been very close ever since. He is a massive hero of mine for everything he has done. It might surprise you that a rugby league player, a prop forward, would be so emotional, but that is me. If something upsets me, I either cry or get angry and in my career I always played with that emotional edge.

***

I was born in Oldham on 8 September 1979 to Linda and Doug. My birth went as simply as any other except I couldn't hold on and ended up being born on the way to the delivery room – I've always been a little impatient. I was eight pounds, six-and-a-half ounces and, according to my dad, was the best behaved of the three sons. I think he must have meant when I was a baby because, when I went to junior school, I was bigger and rougher than everyone else. I did give Mum and Dad some grief when I was younger, though, and Dad tells a story of when I had a tantrum at our local maypole event. In a fit of pique I held my breath until I went from red to blue and then passed out completely and had to be rushed to hospital. The next time I did it my folks knew what was happening and just left me to get on with it. That was a big thing they instilled in all of us – they were not going to wrap us in cotton wool and we had to take responsibility for our own actions. It toughened us up although sometimes we were a little too rough, but it stood us in good stead for the future – and I soon learned that holding my breath didn't work any more!

Whenever we were naughty, Mum would chase us up the stairs with a belt. We would be on our toes, up the stairs as fast as we could and lock ourselves in our room. Then we would be laughing and giving her two fingers behind the door. Despite being small in stature she was the disciplinarian of our parents and we were scared of her. She would say: 'Get your belt off, Doug' and we would be off and running up the stairs. We were too quick for her, though, and we would lean on the door, laughing so she couldn't get in.

One of my earliest memories is of picking peas in the garden at a house nearby in Oldham and then eating them raw. I also remember the Duffel Coat Gang whom we used to have fights with. There were three of them all about the same age as me and my brothers and they only ever wore duffel coats. We would pair off and then have fights and the Sculthorpes always won. We would also play football on the street and get told off by the neighbours. Eventually we ended up moving to Huddersfield Road when I was nine because Dad had had enough of dealing with the problems we caused. Before then I was at Thorpe Primary School, but moving house meant I went to Watersheddings which was the best school for rugby in the area.

When I was little more than a toddler, I used to go to the games when Dad played rugby for Oldham St. Anne's and Shaw, but I never really took an interest in what was happening on the field. I preferred to run around on the sidelines and just do what kids do – have fun and get dirty.

But when I got chance to play the game for real at the age of six, it was clear that it was ideal for me. A chap called Steve Bithell wanted to get kids off the streets and decided to start up a new club in the area called Royton Tigers. My dad saw it advertised in the local paper and decided to take us all down. Lee and Paul were originally playing football, but Dad thought rugby league might be better for them. I tagged along so they could look after me.

We all took to it as if it was the perfect sport! We were allowed to be rough, hit people and get muddy – and we didn't get in trouble for it! I played up for Royton Tigers Under 9s before moving to the same age group at Oldham Juniors – even though I was only seven. My coach Phil McLean was perfect because he would let me score a few tries and then tell me to draw people in, offload and pass. My job after bagging some four-pointers was to set up tries for others. I was bigger than everyone else so it was pointless me running through them for try after try. That did no-one any good so Phil developed my skill in other ways and it helped me to develop as a player. I owe a lot to my coaches Phil, Larry Dawson, Eric Lowther and Mick Hough because they helped me on the way to a successful career. They could see my potential, understood what development I needed and enabled me to play tough and express myself with the ball.

Phil was as daft as a brush. When my Mum and Dad couldn't come and watch me play, I would stay at Phil and his wife Pauline's house on a Saturday night. They would take me to the game and then into the clubhouse where Phil would enjoy several beers and I would wait for Mum and Dad to pick me up. Sunday afternoons followed a similar pattern throughout my junior days. We would end up in

Waterhead Rugby Club and Mum and Dad would enjoy drinking and singing songs with the other parents while the kids would be outside playing rugby with each other. I know it isn't like that today because parents would be worried about where their kids are. But back then they could be in the club for a few hours and they knew their kids were safe. The school holidays were the same. In the summer break my family never saw me because we would all be up at the park spending the full six weeks playing rugby, tennis, football, bulldog and rally-o. All our mates would be there and it would be all sport. Whenever we played rugby it was full tackle. It was absolutely brilliant for us and probably better for Mum and Dad, too, because we wouldn't be fighting at home and breaking cabinets!

I stayed at Oldham Juniors until I played for the Under 10s at nine-years-old and then I moved to Oldham St. Anne's. There we went on tour to Filey in Yorkshire and I got concussed in my first game! But rugby was becoming everything to me and I wanted to play as often as I could. I also wanted to look the part and Christmas always seemed to bring great presents. When we were still young, we would wait for Granddad and Grandma on Christmas morning before we would go downstairs. There would be no sneaking down because we all believed in Father Christmas. We didn't want to spoil the magic because we thought the presents might not have been there or Santa wouldn't come the following year. I remember coming down one morning and getting a pair of Walsh rugby boots. All the kids made fun of me for them because they were just plain black boots, but they didn't realise how much they cost or how comfortable they were. Andy Gregory played in them, but they were clearly not trendy enough for the lads in the team. We always wanted Australian rugby shirts, too, and I remember getting a Cronulla jersey one year. My folks also brought back a rugby ball from the 1988 Challenge Cup final when Saints took on Halifax and I loved it. It was a French rugby ball and was my favourite possession for a long time. My best present ever has to be a bike, though. Every kid wanted a bike, didn't they? It gave me freedom and the chance to spread my wings.

We were probably a little spoilt as kids. Mum and Dad made sure we had everything we needed and we never asked for anything. My grandparents were the same too. Nanna and Granddad (Mum's parents) lived a few miles away in Gorton. Granddad would play pranks and loved jokes and Nanna would serve us salad sandwiches in little wicker baskets. We used to play a game every time we went around to their house. As soon as we got through the door we wanted to play fish, fruit, veg, town, city, country, animal. We would pick a number between one and 26 which would correspond to the alphabet. So three was C. Then you have to pick a fish beginning with that letter, then a fruit and so on. We passed hours playing that game. Grandma and Granddad on Dad's side lived a little further away in Earby and were brilliant, too, and it was always fun to visit them.

It was a massive shock when Granddad Sculthorpe died. The funeral was on Christmas Eve, but I couldn't go because I was too young. I remember the occasion and watching *Chitty Chitty Bang Bang* on the television, but still feeling sad. Grandma Sculthorpe died some years later. I was old enough to attend her funeral in Earby which was an incredibly sad occasion, too. And if that wasn't bad enough, there was a massive snowstorm on the day which caused major problems. Paul and I had gone to Earby with Lee and his wife in their little Renault Five. Paul was playing for Warrington Academy at the time and had a match against Leeds and the intention was to take him on to the game after the funeral. When we got to Leeds the game had been called off, but we didn't know because there were no mobile 'phones back then and he hadn't travelled with his team. It took us four hours to get out of Leeds and then we broke down on the M62. We spent hours pushing other cars and we were all soaking wet and cold. We were freezing and ended up singing rugby songs to keep our spirits up. Paul eventually fell asleep on the back seat so I pinched his skullcap and put it on to try to keep warm. I must have eventually fallen asleep, too, because I remember waking up and there was someone from the RAC knocking on the window and staring at my headgear. He sprayed the engine with WD40 and eventually we got the car started. It was a dreadful day.

It must have been difficult for our parents to kit out three rugby-loving sons who were growing rapidly and wearing it out at a rate of knots, but somehow they managed it. Mum instilled the discipline and taught us the life skills we needed to grow up while Dad was always there for support when we needed it. Sometimes when attending our games he got over-enthusiastic and took this a little too far because there were times when he got pretty mouthy on the touchline! I dreaded him getting wound up because he would start arguing with the ref and other parents, too. In one game I played for Oldham Schoolboys against Wigan, the referee was Ian Ollerton who'd had a successful career officiating in the top flight and is now a match commissioner for the RFL. Wigan were winning when Ian gave a decision Dad didn't agree with so he started mouthing off big style. Ian just said, 'Oi, if you think you can do better, then come on and take over.' He only went and did. He marched on the field, grabbed the whistle and was ready to get the game going. I had to tell him to go away and there's no way he could have kept up with the match! He refereed county trials once and gave a try from halfway because he couldn't keep up. He decided that by staying on the halfway line he would be in place for the kick off.

As I got older and progressed through the junior ranks, I began to meet kids who would become close friends in later life and in some cases teammates. I played with Terry Newton for North Lancashire against South Lancashire at Under 11s in a team who included Paul Deacon, Mike Peters, Martin Carney and Paul Johnson. I played with Stephen Wild at Rose Bridge 14s when I was 12 and then Kevin Sinfield for Oldham Schools at 13. I had some close mates, too. One kid, James Campbell, became my best friend in my teenage years. By then we were both playing rugby for Waterhead and the school. I used to look out for him and make sure he wasn't in any bother because he was a year younger than I was and like a little brother. When I was signed by Rochdale, I used to go out with James and his dad Harry. We would play in a darts and crib team at Waterhead on a Thursday and down plenty of beer, too.

As I was growing up, I was fortunate that people were only too happy to help me develop. When we joined Rose Bridge Rugby Club, near Wigan, Paul and I would go and stay with Ian and Eileen McCulloch who were good friends of our parents and eventually became family after Paul married their daughter Linzi. We would catch the train over for a coaching session on the Saturday and stay over so we were ready to play the day after. They were very good to us in making sure we were okay and ready for the match. Ian coached at Rose Bridge and after Paul had fallen out with Waterhead he suggested to my dad that he should bring him over and I followed soon after. Ian and Eileen are still close friends with our family and are brilliant with our kids, too.

While I was at Rose Bridge I became friends with Linzi's cousin Darren 'Chunk' O'Shea. He was living with Vinny and Marion, Eileen's dad and mum, and, when they went out playing bingo on a Saturday evening, I would stay over with Chunk. The whole McCulloch family really helped us out in our junior days and I'm really grateful for that.

At 11 years of age I moved to Counthill High School in Oldham. I was smart at school – surprising for a prop forward, I know – and I was always in the top sets in different subjects. The school had a good rugby team and we made the National Cup final twice and won the Lancashire Cup. But I didn't enjoy schoolwork; in fact, I hated studying for exams and assessments. I didn't skive off school, but I would always try to feign an illness or say I was feeling sick and often my parents would let me stay off because they were pretty soft with me. I would never do anything behind their backs, though; that isn't how I was brought up. I would never smoke or cause trouble. Okay, I would finish bits of trouble, but never start it. Because I'd stand up to people and wouldn't shy away from a fight, I earned a reputation of being able to look after myself and that stayed with me in my professional career, too. It was never an issue for me, but I think it was for one or two referees.

I remember playing for Oldham against Wigan at St. Jude's. We had good form heading into the game because we had leathered them twice in two previous encounters. In one of those games at Counthill in Oldham it was freezing and we battered them. They were in tears because it was that cold so it was no surprise that at the next game they made sure they got an edge. Professional referee Stuart Cummings came to take charge with two experienced touch judges. He came over to me before the game and said he was watching me. Graeme West was coaching Wigan's side and 20 minutes in I went in hard on his son Dwayne and I was sent off. I didn't do anything! They tried to ban me afterwards, but Joe Warburton, who was running the town teams, said they wouldn't take to the field again if I was disciplined. 'If you ban him then we won't play!' he told the disciplinary meeting the week after the game and I wasn't in the end. What Stuart did was nothing new because I was warned a few times before I took to the field while I was growing up. I wasn't a dirty player, I played to the whistle and just went in hard to put the opposition off their game.

I ended up leaving Counthill High School after about 11 days of my final year. I'd dislocated my knee for Royton Tigers Under 16s at Eccles – the injury that would effectively trigger my diabetes – and had to spent eight weeks away from the place. It had popped during a game and then stayed out. My leg was locked bent and the cap was stuck out to one side. Unfortunately they couldn't get it back into place so I had to go to hospital. I was on gas and air to help with the agony, but by the time I got to accident and emergency it had gone halfway back in, so all they had to do was flick it back into its rightful spot. The doctor got his finger underneath, gave it a tap and then the pain disappeared.

I must have been on the borderline of having type 1 diabetes at the time as the shock of the injury set off a chain reaction. But it wasn't diagnosed until several months later when my weight ballooned and I was having problems. At the time the only problem I had was having a pot on from my ankle to my groin.

At that time I was watching TV one evening with my family when out of the corner of his eye Paul saw someone walking around and messing with his brand new Suzuki Vitara Fatboy outside. He realised they were trying to steal his pride and joy and he and Lee ran out of the house after this chap who legged it around the back. Paul chased after him while Lee went in another direction to head him off. The bloke jumped over a fence only to find Lee waiting for him. They wrestled for a bit until Paul caught up and, when he started hitting out, they gave him a good hiding. I'd made it around the back by then on my crutches and was effecting a swing on my good leg to aim the pot at him. The police eventually got hold of him and he moaned about the treatment he'd received. The copper listened and then whacked him as well for his troubles and he spent a very sore trip in the back of a police wagon to be charged.

When I went back to Counthill one of the principals called me into the office and shut the door behind me. He sat me down and said I'd been causing racial problems and fights. I was shocked at the accusation because it was a downright lie. The school had a lot of Asian kids, just like the town, and there was a lot of tension at the time. There were a lot of racial fights, but it wasn't something I wanted to be involved in so I always stayed clear. I went home and told my Dad what had happened and he was shocked and told me I wasn't going again. As a result I never did my GCSEs and I regret that now. I'm sure I would have done really well and got a load of qualifications, but I didn't because of one principal. The odd thing was, though, despite my self-imposed exile the school never stopped me from playing for them on the rugby field! I probably played 15 times for them during that period. I ended up captaining Lancashire and then England Schoolboys on a tour to France and I wasn't even going to school! Paul had been captain of England the year before so we became the first brothers to have the honour of leading the national side in consecutive years. It was not only an honour for Paul and me, but also for our parents who had put in all the hard work in supporting us. My teachers were big rugby fans, too, and I guess they could see how important it was to me, but they also realised how important I was to them.

***

When I got over my knee injury I was confident I could get back into decent shape and return to form. I played for Royton against Wigan St. Pat's in one game and although we lost 8-6 it was one of the best performances I can remember. I shouldn't have played because my knee hadn't really recovered from the injury, but I wanted to show people I was still around. I scored a try and kicked a conversion off the touchline. Tied 6-6, they went for a drop goal towards the end of the game and I charged it down. Unfortunately I got done for offside and they slotted over the penalty.

I was always a confident player and that game showed that, while my knee wasn't yet fully healed, I could still have a good game. However, I was starting to lose weight which I couldn't figure out. It was some time later when the cause was identified as diabetes. But at the time I was confident that if I kept working hard and playing well I would get signed by a professional club. Some of my teammates had already been offered contracts when I got a call from Leeds Rhinos who said they wanted me to join them on a weekend of training and playing. I knew then that I had a chance. There were about 40 of us on the weekend, including Garreth Carvell and Danny Ward. It was a really intense couple of days that tested how good you really were. We did a huge amount of training followed by a game on the Sunday afternoon when we had to show what we could do. I had a really good game; I saw plenty of the ball, was aggressive and made an impact.

After the game Leeds' chief scout Bob Pickles came over and said he wanted to sign me. He said, 'Go home, tell your parents, and we'll invite you to a meeting at Headingley.' I couldn't wait until I got home so I telephoned Mum and Dad straightaway and they were made up. We met with Bob, coach Dean Bell and one of the directors not long afterwards.

Warrington made it known they were also interested at the time and Brian Gartland the Oldham coach invited me up to the Watersheddings potentially to sign for them, too. It was an amazing feeling to be wanted by so many teams, especially my hometown club. As a kid I looked up to Oldham stars Hugh Waddell and Derek Pyke and I was in awe of players such as Lee Crooks, Kevin Ward and Henderson Gill. I wanted to be like them, play for my country and emulate what they did on the pitch. To be able to be a professional rugby player was my dream and, although Oldham weren't a Leeds or a Warrington, I was flattered by their interest.

Oldham was a community club and their fans were brilliant. Lee, Paul and I would watch the team train on a

Tuesday and Thursday night up at the Watersheddings. We would be playing rugby on the side with our mates on a 10-metre by 10-metre patch of wood chippings – full tackle of course. Funnily there was always a number of odd characters on the sidelines watching, too. One was a chap we called 'Meat Pie Mick' and he would invariably be stuffing a pie into his face. In fact, throughout my time at Rochdale, Meat Pie Mick would be knocking around if Oldham weren't playing and I would catch up and have a good laugh with him. He had a little mate we called 'Gay Alf' because we reckoned they were partners. And there was another chap we named 'Geoffrey Cricket Jumper' who must have been about 40 stone and always wore a massive cricket jumper. And a fourth character whom we called 'Rod Walrus' because he looked like one. He also had a long and greasy mullet. I never spoke to him, but one New Year's Day he came into my local, the Shepherd's Boy. I was with James and Harry Campbell having a big session and Rod Walrus was at the bar supping Newcastle Brown. We invited him over, one thing led to another and we all ended up going out. He got blotto so we bought him a kebab and put him in a taxi. I'm sure he is still watching Oldham now along with Geoffrey in his jumper and Mick scoffing his pie.

When I visited Leeds, they spoke to Dad and me about what they were looking for and offered me £25,000 to sign on. I was blown away because it was far more than I was expecting. I'd heard of players getting decent sums at 16-years-of-age, but never this much and never at Leeds. Wigan and Warrington were supposedly the ones paying the best money. Paul got nothing like that much for joining the Wolves whereas I turned up at Leeds and they offered me £25,000.

I was like: 'Oh my God, where do I sign!'

At the time Paul was already a big success. He had played for Warrington when he was 16 in a side who contained some great players such as Jonathan Davies. He also captained them at 18 before going on tour with the full Great Britain side to New Zealand. He was actually supposed to be on holiday with us at the time I signed on the dotted line for Leeds, but couldn't because he had made the trip Down Under. We sat in a bar and watched him take on the Kiwis, feeling immense pride in what he had achieved at such a young age. It did, however, crank up the pressure on me when I signed for Leeds to try to live up to what he had done.

I was determined to make the best of the opportunity, but my body had other ideas.

3

Million-Pound Player

I didn't suffer any issues after returning from my dislocated knee although I was worried about the long-term effects. I had played well on my comeback and was soon back to full fitness and playing some of my best rugby. I think that form is what led to me being signed by Leeds.

What I hadn't expected was coming out of the injury with diabetes. Apparently people who are borderline with the condition can have it tip them over by a simple event. The trauma of the dislocation had brought on type 1 diabetes which is basically when your pancreas doesn't produce any insulin to use the glucose in your blood to give you energy. Without insulin, the body can't use the sugar in your blood so it resorts to breaking down stores of fat and protein.

There were a number of things happening to my body that, now that I am more aware of the condition, were clear warning signs and classic symptoms of diabetes (the four Ts: Thirsty, Toilet, Tired and Thinner). I was drinking four or five litres of juice every day and going to the toilet several times during the night. I would be watching Paul at Warrington and couldn't see any of the players – I didn't know who was who because of blurred vision caused by dryness of the eyes. But it wasn't until I went up to Barrow for a party and everyone noticed the effect it was having on me that I finally realised something wasn't right. I was a big lad, but I had lost about three stone and they were asking if I was ill. I went to the doctors the following day, peed in a pot and the test showed it was full of ketones, which is a tell-tale sign of diabetes. They appear when the body is burning its own fat and it was clear that was the issue.

I went to hospital and they said my sugars were at 30 whereas they should be between five and eight. I was admitted straightaway, put on insulin and not allowed to leave until everything was under control. I stayed in hospital for a fair old time – something I would become very used to by the end of my career.

A risk of diabetes that people might be aware of is going 'hyperglycaemic' (hypo). It happens when your blood sugars drop to such a level that you can lose consciousness and have convulsions. If it isn't treated quickly, it can lead to death. About this time I was walking down the street one day and began to feel the symptoms of a hypo that quickly got worse. It was frightening as my chest got tighter, it became difficult to breathe and I started to become confused. After that happened I was badly shaken up so I became obsessed with eating carbs to keep my sugars up. The knock-on effect of that was rapid weight gain and I was massive by the time I joined Leeds.

One of the effects of diabetes, especially type 1, is that it can become difficult to lose weight due to thyroid problems and the drugs you have to take. That compounded my problem because the more carbs I ate meant taking more insulin and the weight piled on. It was a vicious circle.

Being overweight is difficult in a sport such as rugby league, especially for a forward. Unlike in Union where there are a few 'larger' players running around, the fact you have to get back 10 yards after each tackle means that the game involves a lot of running and movement. As a result, most players tend to be very lean with a low body fat percentage. There is no hiding place so a hefty, 20-stone guy is going to get found out very quickly. And that is what happened to me.

Unlike today with the examples I set and the advice I can offer to other players, back then I had no support within the game. There were no other rugby league players outwardly diabetic and therefore I had no advice on how to deal with the issues of when to take insulin, what to eat and how to prepare for a match. I'm glad that I can now pass that on to others, but when I first started out it was something I had to deal with myself. I was lucky that my family looked after me and became obsessed with my blood sugars as much as I did. They still do now and, although I just wanted to get on with it myself as a young player, I do appreciate what they did for me.

It all meant a big change to my lifestyle which was hard at first. In the end, I became obsessed with my blood sugars and what level they were at. It wasn't just a case of avoiding them becoming too low; I also had to be careful not to let them to get too high. If that happened and I took insulin, I would get a massive drop in my energy levels which would be a disaster in a match.

***

I joined Leeds on their YTS scheme which is a scholarship now and moved over to the city. That wasn't an easy thing to do because I was a bit of a home-bird, but it needed to be done. I moved in with Phil and Sharon Campbell whose sons Mark and Stephen played for Leeds and Keighley respectively. They were superb with me, but they were as obsessed with feeding me just as much as I was. I put more weight on and needed to do extras to keep that down. I started to do a lot of road running, but that brought on shin-splits which scuppered any training for a while.

I won the Academy Championship with Leeds, but didn't play my best rugby for a number of reasons. I was overweight and living away I was missing my family and friends. At that time I felt some of the symptoms of depression that would catch up with me later in life. I have always been emotional which seems to shock people because I am a rugby league player, but it's who I am. I really felt down and just wanted to be back. In the end Leeds sold me to Warrington as part of the deal that brought Iestyn Harris to Headingley. The Wolves had him on the market for £1,350,000 and he ended up at Leeds for £350,000 plus me. So does that make me the first million-pound player?

I moved back home with my folks and got my head down to make the best of my chance at Warrington. But try as hard as I could, I just couldn't get fit. I was training with the first team, playing for the Academy and also for the A team. Something wasn't right though and I was struggling big time. It was destroying me. I was a good player and the game had always come naturally to me. I was used to dominating on the field, but I couldn't get fit. I tried to train hard, but the weight wouldn't come off. I needed to lose about four stone, but it just wouldn't shift.

Looking back, it was inevitable that I would be released and I suppose it wasn't helped by the fact that Paul had left and signed for Saints. That made the Sculthorpes quite unpopular around Wilderspool! It was a shame because I always loved Warrington. I thought they were a family-friendly club and still do. They have that homely feel and that comes from those days at Wilderspool. The atmosphere after a game was good, the players' bar even better and I would have loved to have played there.

At the age of 14 I would go to all Paul's games at Warrington and be invited into the kit man Ocker's boot room. It was quite a privilege because it was unknown for Ocker to allow anyone into his inner sanctuary. But I was, on the condition I brought him a ham sandwich. And it couldn't be any old rubbish, it had to be fresh bread and best quality ham because he had no teeth. He was a real character, absolutely mad, to be honest. He had a lad there called Tommy helping him out and we became good mates. I have some great memories of my times with Tommy and Ocker. I also became good friends with Kelly Shelford, the New Zealand international. When he was due to return home I went out with all the Kiwis from Warrington and we finished the night off with a pint of Bailey's which was stupid. The morning after he made me an energy drink called Milo which he'd brought from Down Under. Unfortunately my stomach hadn't settled after the Bailey's and I promptly threw up the Milo drink – all over the place!

I still have a soft spot for Warrington from my time at Wilderspool. It's a shame I couldn't play there, but it was understandable. I wasn't fit enough for the Wolves and, when Darryl van de Velde told me they were letting me go, I thought my world was falling apart. In fact, it was probably the best thing that could have happened to me because it gave me the kick up the arse I needed.

4

Buzzing at the Hornets

Mixing plaster for eight hours a day at a tenner a pop was hardly the career I expected to be in when I signed for Leeds and then Warrington. After being released, I was hoping to be snapped up by another Super League club, but I needed to keep myself busy and earn a few quid. Working for Pete 'Bully' Byrne, a chap who once coached me at Waterhead, was ideal because it helped with my fitness and the money came in handy for the pub. It was glorified slave labour, though, because I was mixing plaster with a shovel all day long for dry lining. Eventually my brother Lee came to my rescue and asked if I wanted a labouring job at a sheet metal factory for a few more quid. It was a simple choice and the blokes I worked with were superb. They were all older than I was, but they were a good, fun bunch and the banter was hilarious. It was a really physical job, moving sheet metal around, drilling and painting, and it coincided with an unexpected offer from a teacher at North Chadderton whom I had known from growing up.

I'd known Iain 'Corky' MacCorquodale throughout my amateur career. My school and his were always competing against each other. I also helped him to sell raffle tickets at Oldham Roughyeds – I cleaned up with my selling technique if I am honest! – and we became good mates. When he heard I had been released by Warrington, he asked around to find out if I had signed anywhere else. When he found out I was a free agent, he asked me if I wanted to go and train at Rochdale where he was on the coaching staff. I was trying to get in some kind of shape so it made sense to go over there and see where it went. And I wanted to get fit, so, if a call came from a club, I would be in good enough condition to take it up – or at least impress on trial.

Moving back home gave me the opportunity to look closely at my diet and working with Lee had the added effect of me taking more care of what I ate. As the gopher I would do all the runs to the shop for breakfast and dinner. Lee would have spam, cheese and tomato on toast every morning whereas I would start the day with a grapefruit. And if they went to the chippy at dinner time, I would make do with a salad. It was a real ball-ache to be fair, but it worked and gradually the weight began to come off. Added to which, if I wasn't working, then every opportunity I had I would be down at Waterhead doing extras with some of the guys there which sharpened up my fitness. I would train with a chap called Ken Wilson, an ex-Marine who would put me through hell. He never took his training gear home … he would wear it, sweat buckets and then put it back in a bag in the changing rooms. Next time he came in, it would be taken out of the bag and put back on. It certainly made me run harder to try to keep a bit of distance between us!

When I joined Rochdale, I didn't expect a lot and I have to admit I was disappointed at ending up there. Growing up, I wanted to play for the best in the country and I'd been on a high when first Leeds and then Warrington had signed me. But at 19-years-of-age it felt as if I had dropped down through a trap-door because the Hornets weren't even a big club in the Championship. However, it turned out to be the best thing that could have happened. My first session with my new teammates was on a field at a school. We were knee-deep in mud and working our butts off, but it was a laugh as well and I felt comfortable from day one. Corky was caretaker coach at the time, taking over from Shane Tupaea, and I seemed to fit in well with him and his style.

Eventually I played Academy, A team and then first team for Rochdale – and some of that was during the course of one weekend! I am one of those blokes who would get fit by playing and it did wonders for me. I enjoyed playing long minutes with the ball in hand and giving people a crack. With my better diet, the extras I was doing and playing plenty of games, I was in the sort of condition I wanted to be and it reflected on the field.

Off the pitch I was still working with Lee and really enjoying it. The factory owner Ken was good to us all. His wife also had type 1 diabetes so he understood my problems if I went hypo. He also gave me lots of advice on how to manage my condition and it was really helpful to get insights from someone who knew about diabetes.

While I was at the factory, I became pretty close to an old chap called Burt Rothwell. He drove an old Reliant three wheel car like Del Boy's and I would spend lunch breaks with him while he ate his home-made pea and ham soup. I would make all the brews and make sure his was the best! I wanted to look after him because he was great with me. Burt ended up using my Mum and Dad's caravan at Fleetwood too. He was a welder in his early 60s and a proper old man in his attitude. If we got a big job, he would take charge and oversee it. Once it was done he would shout: 'Normal duties' and we would all return to our stations.

At Rochdale I played for a couple of weeks in the Academy and then eight weeks in the A team to get up to speed and fitness. After that I made my full debut for the Hornets. A-team rugby doesn't really exist any more and it's a shame because that was where many players cut their teeth before stepping up to the full squad. I also had the opportunity to play alongside Lee there. One time we played against Widnes and they had a really strong team. The likes of Simon Knox and Dave Bradbury turned out for them while Lee was at stand-off and I was at prop for the Hornets. We also had a chap called Paul Geener with us. He was a mate from Waterhead and we called him in because we were down on numbers. He came on to play in the second row after someone got injured even though he normally played as a centre or winger.

We lost the game, but won every fight. I like to mix it up, Lee likes to play it rough and Geener was downright filthy. In one tackle I was punching, Lee was pulling and Geener was gouging. It was like that all through the game and we got away with it. Lee and I played together for the first team a couple of times, too, and one at Sheffield Eagles sticks in the memory because we beat them on the last play of the last set of six of the game. Lee passed to me and I chipped over for our winger Marlon Miller to turn it back inside for our centre who went in under the posts. That was Lee's debut for the Hornets and I got man of the match. They were special times that will never leave me.

I made my debut for Rochdale on 24 June 1998. I was

training with the first team on the Saturday and got the nod from new coach Deryck Fox that I was in line to make the bench for the game the following Wednesday. It was exciting, but I was crapping myself because it was away at Whitehaven and they were a tough, horrible team. Travelling up there is a hell of a journey and a tough place for a kid to go to make his bow. I remember being very nervous and not playing a lot of minutes. I came on for the last 20, but it was a good start for me although we lost 24-6. I don't think there was a tougher place to play than Whitehaven back then other than maybe a visit to Featherstone. Rugby in the Championship at that time was tough, rough and really dirty. I remember getting properly beaten up playing against Featherstone and to add insult to injury we lost! I played twice off the bench in 1998 and the following year 23 times.

The Championship suited my skill set because I liked to play on the edge. It wasn't fast, but it was hard. When I came from the A team, I was still carrying a bit of weight, but I soon got up to the speed of the game and felt pretty comfortable. I was a niggly player and I wouldn't let anyone bully me or the team and the Championship suited that style. I also had a little more time with the ball and that meant I could show what I could do. Every coach at Rochdale allowed me to express myself on the field and I am thankful for that. I played tough when I needed to and I was allowed to get involved properly in the attack. I played like a stand-off at Rochdale, albeit an overweight one, and I think that is what eventually led to my move into Super League.

The thing about Rochdale in my time there was the camaraderie and team spirit. It was unbelievable. We would work hard in training, spend time together afterwards and head to the clubhouse after a game. And no matter what happened we all got on. No-one would fire off or become a loose cannon or cause problems. The game was done and that was it. It was a homely club from top to bottom. We were all welcome back at the clubhouse and once we'd had a decent session we would all head out to Oldham for a night out. When you have happy players, they play better and that is why I played well at Rochdale.

The chairman Ray Taylor was a top man and anything we needed he would find. Director Tony Pratt would come into the dressing room at half time if we were losing and say there's a brown envelope for a few drinks if you go on to win this! Such things make you want to play for a club and it was an awesome place to be around. There were some characters, too. Mark Reynolds was the kitman at the Hornets and a decent guy, but if you didn't know him, you'd think he was a bad-tempered sod. He was very easily wound up and often got sent off when we were playing for shouting abuse at the referees. The lads were also pretty ruthless at times. I used to keep a bottle of Lucozade handy when I was training in the gym. One morning I'd hammered the rowing machine and grabbed the bottle for a swig, only to find someone had pissed in it! I also remember someone dropping a turd and trying to ignite it with a cigarette lighter which was pretty grim! Players are a different breed sometimes and do things no-one else would even think of.

Anyway I had some legendary sessions throughout my time at Rochdale with my teammates and friends from Oldham and Waterhead. I would be playing darts, crib and dominoes at Waterhead, go out on Friday with my mates, stay in on Saturday and then smash it all day Sunday. That continued for a while and, looking back, I don't know how I did or how my body coped.

Early on I probably struggled with not knowing exactly what booze did to my diabetes and I got myself into a little trouble. I'd drink too much and then get mouthy, but thankfully it didn't happen too often. I fell out with Paul one Christmas because I was convinced his wife Linzi didn't want me at their house. It was total bollocks, of course, but that is what the booze did to me – especially lager. My emotional mind would work on overload. Another time when I had too many beers, I ended up wrestling with one of my mates in a pub. We were going at it pretty hard when he slipped and split his head on a radiator. It was an accident and we went to the toilets to get cleaned up. Suddenly he started calling me, saying I was too rough and a bully. I didn't like that and, like a switch being flicked in my head, I snapped and ended up smashing all the windows in the toilets. I stomped out of the bar and got a little way down Yorkshire Street, but then got even angrier and decided to head back in for seconds. When I got back, I noticed my hands were covered in cuts so I went into the toilet to sort them out. But the bouncers got hold of me and called the police. I was cautioned for that one and quite rightly, too, as I was when I was in the Shepherd's Boy, my local, not long afterwards.

The incident in the Shepherd's Boy that got me in bother concerned a former soldier who was having a few beers in there and was picking on some of my mates. He'd had a few too many and was calling them shit rugby players. I told him to stop and to his credit he did. However, he just decided to start on me instead. I couldn't cope with that so put my drink down, walked over and whacked him. He flew across the pub, hit the jukebox and I followed to give him a leathering on the floor. Once it had died down he got kicked out because the landlady knew it was his fault. My mates and I stayed in the pub for a couple more hours until we decided to walk home. We were heading to Mum and Dad's house and the ex-soldier was waiting for us. There were a few insults hurled back and forth, but otherwise nothing happened until one of the lads I was with said we were walking past his house. Like an idiot I grabbed a brick and threw it through his window. Problem was, it wasn't his house. I had woken this couple up and they were going mental. It turned out they called the police who caught up with me just before I got home. I held my hands up and admitted what I'd done, but the lads I was with had disappeared so I got cautioned again.

Most of the time I was sensible in terms of avoiding trouble and could just show off with my drinking prowess. On a good-day session I could do 30 pints easily which was ridiculous considering I have diabetes. After an A team game against London I met a couple of the Waterhead boys – Nick Wood and Danny Parkin – who had played against me for the Broncos that day. We met in the Shepherd and my brother Lee came out, too. He was there for only about three hours and I had 19 pints of Guinness in that time. Lee did about 17 and had hidden some behind some books and a plant pot. He left about 11.00pm and said he fell over everyone's wheelie bins on the way back to his house. I was still sat in the pub at 7.00 the next morning, eating toast with a Guinness.

I also hold the record around those parts for the yard of ale. Recently I went up to the Lake District and met a guy I played with at Rochdale called Chris McKinney who is now the coach of Hensingham, an amateur club near Whitehaven. They were playing Ellenborough in a top-of-the-table clash and after their game it is customary for the man of the match to do the 'yard'. The away recipient stepped forward and downed his in about three-and-a-half minutes. Off the glass went to the bar for a refill and I had a funny feeling what was coming next. Chris got on the microphone and said, 'We have some friends here today from a local team in Wigan called the Ashton Bears. Can you pick one of your best drinkers to do the yard of ale for us?' Chris had obviously had a word with all the parents at the Bears and they pushed me forward. I stood up, grabbed the glass and downed all two-and-a-half pints in 11 seconds. The pub record up to that point was 13.

I did the yard in 12 seconds on my stag do. We'd been at Wetherby races and also around Leeds, but returned home the day after to continue the celebrations. They had already stripped me off and wrapped me in cling film, leaving me in a pair of Caterpillar boots and nothing else. I wouldn't have minded normally because rugby blokes like getting their kit off, but it was freezing as it was December! When the yard of ale came out, I smashed the pub record by 24 seconds, but it didn't stay in me long and I ran outside and was sick on this bloke's Christmas trees. Understandably the sight of seeing someone dressed in cling film, hurling over trees that he was selling, didn't fill him with festive spirit and he had a right go at me. Afterwards I made my way back in and the boys had got me a stein of Guinness which was great because I was now empty and ready to go again. The barman said he would race me with a glass of the black stuff, too, and I duly beat him!

Pretty much all I did in my early career was hit the beer

somewhere and then come back home. If we played on a Friday, after the game I would head up to my folks' caravan in Fleetwood for the weekend, go around there or Blackpool and then come back home. Failing that, I would be at the Waterhead Rugby Club with some great lads I will always be mates with. The likes of John Eastwood, Steve McDonald, Ste Whitmore, Ganz, Craig Mort and Paddy Mitchell will be friends forever. We'd also head to Austerlands Cricket Club because we knew it would be open once Oldham closed on a Sunday night. I'd get out of there on a Monday morning at about 6.00am, have about 30 minutes' sleep and then drive to work. Those mornings were a total write-off. I would turn up, make everyone a brew and then go hiding. I'd be in the toilets asleep until it was time to ask what they wanted for breakfast. I would go and do that, deliver the goods and then be back in the toilets until 11.00am. It was then time to see what they wanted from the chippy! I'd be at the chip shop for 11.15, get an hour or so in my car until I had to pick up the food and then be back to work. I was usually in a fit state by then to have a go at some real graft.

Another food run I had to complete upon pain of death was the end-of-night kebab run. Every time I went out, I would never ever go home without a kebab for my Dad. It was an unwritten law. There were several different kebabs he really liked. The 99p special from the Gold Star was gorgeous, but it was small so I had to take him a couple back. They also did a number six which was the size of a sleeping bag. If I was feeling a little flush or I'd had a good game, I would go to Number 91, the takeaway which was next door to the Scruples Nightclub in Oldham. Those beauties would come in a tray filled with pitta bread, chips, lamb, chicken, loads of sauce and salad. I think it was called a makhlout kebab. On returning home, no matter what the time, I would head upstairs and wake him up. He would sit up, bleary-eyed and eat his kebab. If I'd got him one of the specials, he'd eat half there and then and tuck in again in the morning … and the remainder for tea later. I reckon that's why he ended up being about 26 stone at one point!

Whenever I was in the pub I had this thing for gambling machines. I would spend 30 or 40 quid in them and, added to what I was supping, it was getting out of hand financially. So I came up with a unique way of solving my addiction. I bought my own gambling machine and put it in my bedroom at home. It worked, too, because after a while I got bored with the pay-out level set to near impossible. It was good for saving up in that respect and shortly afterwards I got shut of it.

The closeness at Rochdale and the bond we all had as teammates meant that, when tragedy struck, we felt it even more. We lost Karl Marriott at just 28-years-old in October 1998 and then Deryck's assistant Roy Powell a couple of months later. It was totally devastating. Karl was a tough player and super fit. We had finished a gym session before having a competition on the rower to see how fast we could complete 1,000 metres. I did mine in three minutes 11 seconds, the Best twins (David and Jason) then had a go and Karl was last up. He was blowing when he finished, like we all were, but was fine and went home. Sadly, he died of a massive heart attack that evening. It struck us all hard because he was a good friend as well as a teammate.

Tragedy hit us again a couple of months later when Roy Powell died in similar circumstances. We were doing a drill called 'Malcolms'. You start on the 10-metre line, run up ten and hit the floor before going back 20 metres and hitting the deck again. That is classed as one rep and the idea is to do six at a time for 90 seconds. I was running at the side of him and all seemed to be going well until I heard a thud as he hit the floor. I knew something was wrong straightaway so I immediately went back, dropped down and turned him over. Roy was biting his lip and I could see something was seriously wrong. One of the lads tried to give him mouth-to-mouth, but because he was biting his lip he couldn't get air in. The ambulance came after about 20 minutes and took him to hospital, but he never made it through. He was just 33.

It was another tragedy that hit us all hard. We had a tough training session a couple of weeks later on the dunes in Southport and I remember Stephen Wild shouting at Foxy: 'Fucking hell, you will kill us here.' Foxy didn't like that for obvious reasons even though Wildy didn't mean it. Words like that cut Foxy deep because he was best mates with Roy who was not only a top player for us, but his assistant, too. Like Karl, Roy was really fit. He was probably the fittest in the team, but had something wrong with his heart.

Deryck was a top coach. Whatever we did in training, he would be right in there doing the same. He did what we did and more. He was as fit as a fiddle and strong in the gym, too, and, as a result, was a tough taskmaster. He could lose his rag if you weren't doing well, but praise you if you did something good. We all wanted to play for him because he put his body on the line on and off the field. He played scrum-half in 1999 for us and would always get me involved in the attacking plays. It was good to learn from someone who had played 14 times for Great Britain so it was a real shame when he moved on in June that year. I suppose the owners made the decision because we hadn't won a lot of games, but the bond at the club was strong and we had been through a lot together.

Bob Eccles came in as a caretaker coach from Crosfields in Warrington and he was another good, down-to-earth coach. Like Deryck he'd played at the highest level – with Warrington – and appeared for his country, so he had great experience to draw on when he coached us. But Bob left in November and Steve Linnane took over. He had played for St George in the NRL and probably knew more than Corky, Foxy and Eccles about the game. He was a good man-manager and got the best out of the players, myself included. I was getting myself to a high level of fitness at that time and my form was good, too, which led to signing a new contract. I went from match payments only to a guaranteed £5,000 a year which was a lot of money for me back then. It still meant I had to work at the factory with Lee, but I could afford the better kebabs for big Doug. It was a new millennium and probably the moment I realised I was going to carve a living from the game. Incidentally I celebrated the big 2000 date at a huge party on Paul's street. We set up a marquee with Paul's neighbours – Oldham coach Mike Ford, his wife Sally Anne and their three sons – and Dad got legless on whisky because he had a cold! So he says …

I played 22 games that 2000 season, got picked for the Championship Dream Team and was in the running for Player of the Year, too. But I was also beginning to feel paranoid because Steve moved on in June to become assistant coach at Halifax. I'd worked with four coaches in three-and-a-bit seasons at Rochdale! Before he left he brought in Shayne McMenemy from Western Suburbs and Dane Dorahy. But it didn't work out for Shayne and he was let go. Rochdale wouldn't let him sign for another team over here, so Linnane drove him to the airport to head home. But he didn't go home! Once Steve had gone I picked Shayne up from the airport and he ended up living with me for about six months! He eventually signed for Oldham and we ended up playing against each other in a number of games including the Law Cup. We became like brothers and I was best man at his wedding. He married Rochdale's physio Alison when he signed for Halifax in Super League. I reckon I saved his career by bundling him out of the airport and, in effect, set up his marriage, too. Only joking, Shayne ... but all this happened without Rochdale knowing.

When Steve left the club, they brought in Steve Deakin who – would you have guessed it? – didn't stay for two months before he went the way of the others! He rejoined Keighley as head coach and Martin Hall took over in November. Thankfully things settled down then and Martin eventually took us to two consecutive third-place finishes in the Northern Ford Premiership and within a snip of promotion.

Having so many coaches in such a short time caused a lot of disruption, but I was young and just wanted to play so it didn't really matter to me who was in charge. But as Hall got the chance to be there longer than the others, we became a more settled team and made a semifinal in the Premiership play-offs in 2001. We played Oldham in that semi and were very close to being promoted. Games against the Roughyeds were always tough old ties. It was usually full bore and no holds barred. We were well up in the contest, but Mike Ford came on for them and changed the game. We were literally minutes away from the Grand Final, but he worked his magic and we lost 39-32. There's no way we should have lost the game and it was very disappointing, but we just couldn't live with Fordy. We blew it because the Grand Final would have been against Widnes at Spotland, our home ground. We had beaten them already that year and I'm sure we would have done again. Rochdale in the Super League would have been fucking mad, but it sadly didn't happen. If it had, who knows where I would be today?

Towards the end of my time at Rochdale I got picked to tour South Africa with England Under 21s. It came after I impressed in a game where a Premiership select team faced a Super League select. I was called up to play in the Premiership team and the idea was the selectors would choose the Under 21 squad from whoever did well. The Premiership players had the upper hand because most were first-team regulars, whereas the Super League lads were predominantly Academy and A teamers. We played against them at Widnes and absolutely smashed them across the park. I was propping with Gareth Haggerty and we bullied them. Wigan's Ricky Bibey was telling everyone in the build-up what he was going to do to me and there was no way I was going to let him get the better of our clash. He thought he was a real hard man, but in the first scrum I gave it to him and from there we beat them up.

Ridiculous as it sounds, after we got the better of the Super League boys, only four players from the Premiership got selected to tour. John Kear picked me, Neil Turley, Rob Purdham and Paul Salmon to travel. We had a couple of training camps before we went out and at the final one Kear pulled me and Ryan Hudson to one side and said Ryan would be captain and I would be vice-captain. I was given the honour over the likes of Danny McGuire, Rob Burrow, Chev Walker and Keith Mason who were Super League players and it was an unbelievable feeling.

We went out there, did well and it was a fantastic experience. Ryan captained in the first Test, but didn't play in the second so I was made captain. That was a massive honour, not only for me but Rochdale, too, and I made sure afterwards I gave my shirt to the chairman, Ray Taylor, as a thank-you for what the club had done to enable me to get there.

Before we came home we stopped off at Sun City. Kear had put us on a booze ban, but it wasn't long before it was ignored. I and several others decided to head off for a drink. We'd had a few when Jerry Springer walked through the bar! We all started chanting 'Jerry, Jerry' and he came over for a chat. We asked him why he was there and he said he was judging Miss World. Then all the Miss World candidates strolled through, too! You don't need to give a load of pissed-up rugby players a chance like that, but we weren't allowed too close because they were protected by bodyguards! That was a shame, but it underlined what a cool trip it was. Ben Westwood was a pain throughout while Rob Parker kidnapped four ducks and had them in a bath. Kear didn't like this sort of behaviour and was not impressed. I don't think he had much of a sense of humour and he wouldn't speak to any players apart from myself and Ryan. It was always: 'Danny, could you have a word with ...?' and that lasted for the entire two weeks.

When I got back, I was approached by Wigan and London Broncos to sign with them and go fully pro. The CEO from the Broncos came up and spoke to me, my Mum and Dad, but I wasn't too keen on going down to London because it would have meant moving away from my family and the bad experience at Leeds was still fresh in my mind. I nearly signed for London as a free agent in 2006 when Cas had been relegated and Brian McDermott sold it to me, but I turned it down because I still didn't want to move south. When Wigan came in, it was a no-brainer. I met Maurice Lindsay, he told me what they were offering and I signed straightaway on a three-year contract. It was worth £35,000 in the first season and would increase by five grand each year. I was only on five grand at Rochdale as well as working at the sheet metal place to top that up so I couldn't turn it down. It meant I could go full-time, too.

I played 83 times for Rochdale and I cannot express how good they were to me. I loved my time there and they put a lot of faith in me after I was released by Leeds and Warrington. They gave me my chance and I grabbed it with both hands. The deal was good for them, too, because they got a big transfer fee which basically saved them from going under. Whatever coaching, time, effort and friendship they put into me I gave back in that deal. At our end-of-season dinner I made a speech in the clubhouse – as Player of the Year – and Ray gave me a Rolex for my 21st birthday and a cheque. It was hard doing that speech because I knew I was on my way, but it hadn't been officially announced. That came in December 2001. I was proud to play for the Hornets and more so for Ray. When he died, his wife Barbara gave me back the England shirt and it is now in my son's bedroom. I look at it now and again and it still says 'To Ray' on it. At his funeral I was honoured to be asked to be one of his coffin-bearers alongside Bobbie Goulding.

Rochdale saved my rugby-league career by showing

faith in me and allowing me to express myself on and off the field, which enabled me to move on after the disappointment of Leeds and Warrington. Now it was time to make a big step up and prove that they had been right.

5

Warrior

I'd like to take issue with the phrase: 'Behind every great man is a great woman'.

I met my Nat in 2001 and I love her to bits. She has been there through thick and thin, the highs, lows and hypos of my career, and the depression. But I'm no great man. I'm humble, understand where I have come from and owe everything to my family. I'd like to rephrase it to: 'Behind every great woman is a Danny Sculthorpe who is batting way above his average!' Doesn't exactly trip off the tongue, but it's more than true.

I knew Nat a long time before we actually got together. She was with my good friend Jason Best and had moved in with him. They had been together practically from school. She would come and drop 'Besty' off on our nights out and I would say 'hello' and wonder how they had ended up together. When they split, I mithered her to death to go out with me. Mostly drunk I would lay on the charm, be cheeky and hope one day she would say 'yes.' Thankfully she did. We got married four years later and now have three great kids.

I'd been trying to get Nat to go out with me for ages until a mate and I ended up meeting her and her cousin

Carla in a pub on a Wednesday night in Oldham. I was downing the pints and laying it on pretty thick when she decided to take Carla home because she was driving. My mate disappeared, too, and then not long afterwards Nat came back into the pub. We got chatting once again and I invited her – it's not very classy – to come to Blackpool with me. I'd asked a few times before, but I'd always got a flat 'no' because I was usually pissed. She finally relented, but I was seeing someone at the time so I had to come up with a plan. I told my girlfriend I was going on a stag do to Cleethorpes with my mates and ended up heading up the M6 to Blackpool with Nat. We stayed in the Lindene Hotel in Blackpool and had a great night out watching comedian Mick Miller.

Nat told me before we went that there would be no naughty stuff – I was on a sex ban basically – but being a fairly typical bloke I didn't want to waste any opportunity! I booked a family room, but I think Nat expected two single rooms. I said the hotel must have made a mistake (ahem), but in the end we finished up putting the two single beds together in the room. We obviously clicked, so when I got home I ended my relationship. I told my then girlfriend I needed to concentrate on my rugby and I know she was pretty upset.

The first time I took Nat out 'officially' was also the first time she met Mum and Dad. But the relationship very nearly ended before it began! I'd spent all day in Waterhead Rugby Club and, after 20 bottles of Becks, decided I would pick her up and take her for a meal. I pulled my car up to her house and once we were on the A627 coming out of Oldham she realised I had been drinking. She said I'd ruined it and told me to turn around and take her home. And rightly so! I ended up taking her to my folks' house, we had a brew and ended up talking for hours. She then practically moved in with us. She would be around all the time and became part of the family.

It took until Christmas Eve 2004 before I decided to pop the question. I got down on one knee in the front room of our house and asked her if she would marry me. Gladly she said 'yes' and we got married on 10 December 2005, just months after I had been released by Wigan. It can't have been easy for Nat considering I was often pissed and a bit of an idiot, but she stuck with me. Perhaps that is what charmed her in the first place.

Starting to date Nat coincided with joining Wigan and taking a massive step forward in my career. I was now a full-time professional, but it probably didn't dawn on me what that entailed until much later at the Warriors. I was the same relaxed bloke who was going on two-day benders at the weekend and it took me a while to realise I couldn't do that any more if I wanted to be successful. For a start, we trained as much at Wigan in one day as we had done in a week at Rochdale. Everything was miles faster, even in training, and those little games and tests on the training field were really hard. I don't want to belittle Rochdale because the training there had been tough, but it had nothing on the standards at Wigan! During pre-season we did lots of running and that was a bit of shock. We went to Cyprus for pre-season, too, and that was just brutal with double sessions and more running.

On returning to Wigan, I was in the gym squatting weights with Harvey Howard when I prolapsed a disc. I probably went a little too heavy and on the third rep felt a sharp pain in my back. I stopped immediately, but a few weeks later I got really bad sciatic pain and I knew something wasn't right. Wigan used the 3G Soccerdome pitches to train on and I couldn't run on them because of the pain, so I asked the doctor to check it out. After various scans and check-ups they decided I needed a discectomy and laminectomy, both major procedures. The former involves removing part of a disc in your back to relieve the pressure on your spine, while the latter cuts some of the bone away to allow nerves to move and be free. As would become pretty typical for me there was a fuck-up afterwards because my stitches burst in recovery so I had to go back into surgery. Once that was done, things seemed pretty normal until the area around the wound began to swell because of internal bleeding. That meant I was back on the table for my third operation in four hours. That's me all over really, nothing is simple and I had to have a drain fitted in my back to remove all the shit and blood.

The club's physio, Alan Tomlinson, was superb with my recovery and sent Emma Fletcher, one of his staff, to watch the operation so they would know what was going on. Alan also structured a new weights programme when I returned and organised an intensive physio programme which got me back playing. Wigan were nothing but superb with me and I am thankful for that. It must have been frustrating for them seeing one of their new signings injured before having a chance to make his debut, but that is the nature of our sport. They were looking after their investment and, in doing so, ensuring I got the best treatment. Stuart Raper was my coach and he was excellent with me, as was the club during my long rehab. They made sure I was very much part of day-to-day life at the Warriors and took me to the Challenge Cup final at Murrayfield where we beat Saints

21-12. I went to the game with other players who missed out and their wives and watched the game with Nat in the stands.

The night of the win was superb; we partied until the early hours and there was a lot of head-shaving going on. The next day the squad went back to Wigan for the homecoming, but I didn't go on the bus. The lads did ask me to join them, but I was cheesed off that I had missed the game. It was horrible coming back with the players' wives knowing what would be happening on the other bus, but I felt that, because I hadn't played a part in the victory, it would have been wrong for me to get involved. Dave Whelan gave the team £25,000 for winning the cup, too, and, because I was in the 25-man squad, I got a grand despite not even playing a game. That was a nice bonus, but I would have loved to have played in the game. Sean O'Loughlin missed out and Ricky Bibey was in as a result. I was confident I would have got in before him!

***

Once I got back to fitness and close to playing, Stuart suggested I went out on loan to get properly match-fit. He said I could choose between Whitehaven – because Dean Bell's dad was coaching there – or my former club Rochdale. It made sense to head back to the Hornets because I knew I would be comfortable there and would be able to give of my best. I went on to play three games for them and the first – my first after nine months – was at Lancashire Lynx coached by Graeme West. It felt like I had never been away as we battered them and I played really well. Another two games followed before Wigan called me back and I was handed my debut against Saints at home on 8 September 2002, my birthday.

I had a celebratory meal with my family for my 23rd at Crimble Hall in Rochdale and Paul asked me if I would be playing because he knew I was now back at Wigan. Stuart told me not to tell anyone, not even my folks. I didn't want to betray his trust so I played dumb. On the 8th I travelled to the game with Paul with my bag in his boot. He kept on asking if I was going to play because I had my gear with me, but I said, 'No, I was only 18th or 19th man.' I would have loved to have seen his face when the team sheet was handed into the Saints' dressing room about an hour before the game! It was a 25,000 sell-out at the JJB Stadium as it was then called and I played the last 20 minutes. It was so fast, frighteningly fast, and I did bugger all. I spent the time trying to get used to the speed of the game and also to try to soak it all in. The atmosphere was superb and we smashed them 48-8 which made it an unbelievable debut.

I ended up playing the rest of the season for the Warriors – another six games – and in the final one Saints got some revenge by knocking us out of the play-offs 24-8 to get to the Grand Final. They went on to win it against Bradford and I was chuffed to bits for Paul. He was really supportive of me joining Wigan and said I should take full advantage of what was coming. If Saints had come in with the same offer, I would have gone there for sure because I would have loved to have played alongside him. I watched the way he carried himself throughout his career and his dedication was an inspiration because it showed what I had to do to play in Super League. I would always be classed as Paul's brother, but I didn't give a shit about that. Why would I? Paul was a class player so to be associated with him is a no-brainer. I was never jealous one bit. That said, when the Wigan fans sang, 'There's only one decent Sculthorpe,' that did piss me off until I realised it was about me.

The back end of 2002 felt good. The year before I had been at Rochdale and lost in that semifinal to Oldham. Had we won that game, I am convinced we would have gone on to beat Widnes in the Grand Final and been promoted to Super League. If that had happened, maybe I would have stayed at the Hornets. But as it worked out, Rochdale got a big transfer fee for me which saved them from going under, so I guess I did right by them.

I was on a high as the season closed. It had been a long journey via Leeds, Warrington and Rochdale to make my debut in Super League. And I'd had to overcome setbacks with a knee dislocation, back surgery and diabetes, but it had been worth it for the breakthrough.

I kicked on in 2003 and had a great year. It came on the back of having a very good pre-season and getting up to speed with Super League. Although I damaged my sternum in the gym and played with injections for the first eight weeks, it didn't damage my form and I stayed in the side. Nor did the unexpected dental cock-up that saw me breaking a bone in my gum. I'd been having trouble with my teeth, but hadn't been for a check-up for so long that I had been dropped by my local dentist. I ended up going to a practice near Manchester. I went in, showed the dentist the problem and he said it had to come out straightaway. He numbed the gum, got to work and I braced myself as he started to pull the tooth out. When it finally came out, I heard a big snap. I assumed that was pretty normal and just the root breaking free. Once I got cleaned up I asked him how much the procedure was and he told me not to worry about it. That set some alarm bells off, but, because the work had been done, I didn't think much more about it. How stupid was I?

Once the numbness wore off I was hit with a tremendous pain and one side of my head was in bits. After a while it got too much, so I went back to the dentist to see what had happened. He checked it over and said everything was fine so I thought it was just fall-out from the procedure and went off to training. But it gradually got worse so I ended up going to Wigan Warriors' dentist, Barry Rimmer, in Ashton. He took one look and said that, when the dentist had removed the tooth, he had broken the bone underneath. Ah, so that was the snap! Barry fixed it for me and my mum called the offending dentist a number of times to say we were going to sue him! We didn't, but we let him know he'd made a mess of me. He had basically ripped the tooth out with so much force that it snapped a piece off the bone. I can still feel that now.

**

Stuart Raper liked my style of play and never tried to change what I was on the field. I have to admit it was difficult to be the type of player I was at Rochdale because of the sheer quality we had at Wigan. If I was to put a kick in at Wigan with Faz (Andy Farrell) on the field, he would have blasted me. Any players who came in from overseas struggled to impose their game and style on the side because, if Faz wanted the ball, he would get it. It worked at times, of course it did, because Faz was world-class, but it was hard for other players to show what they could do. He would dominate the ball and do 25 hit-ups, all the kicks and things like that, and was so good at it. It perhaps put other players off, but you couldn't really complain because he was so talented.

Faz was the ultimate pro and, by following his lead, it made me a better player. If we had a session starting at 8.00am, he would be in training at 7.00am doing his warm-up exercises and then stretching so that when the rest of the boys came in he was ready to go. I did what he did and worked out with conditioner Nigel Ashley-Jones. I also did boxing with Craig Smith and Dave Furner which helped me to build my fitness and stay in the team.

I played 24 times for Wigan that season, scoring five tries. I also got capped once for Lancashire and four times for England A against Australia and in the Euro Nations. I continued to be as aggressive as I could be and that helped me massively, especially as a forward. I always needed to get over the top of my opposition. At the first scrum I would test them out by going in hard and with the head. As a result I knew from the outset what sort of game I was in for. If my opposite number gave it back, it was fair play and I knew I was in for a tough game. If I gave it to them and they didn't fight back, then I knew I had an edge on them from the start. It was always my style to start a game that way so I knew what I would be dealing with for the rest of the match

There was a time when this approach got my teammates into a little trouble as, against Leeds, I managed to smash Faz's nose across his face in a tackle. Kevin Sinfield took the ball in and I wanted to hurt him because he was their best player. We'd played together at school, but this was different! Faz went in low and, as I came in, I caught him square in the face with my knee. Faz's nose took the impact, there was blood everywhere and he had to leave the pitch.

But Faz being Faz he strapped it up, came back on and put in a superb performance which helped us to win the game.

It's true that sometimes I would go over the top and try too hard or be reckless and that was probably more evident when I played against St. Helens. I wanted to go out and hurt them rather than play rugby and sometimes that spoiled my game. When I was playing and being aggressive, most of the time it really helped. I wasn't just a thug; I could also play. At Rochdale players would call me a scrum-half in a prop's body. I could pass, kick, offload and read a game. But if I let my aggression get out of control, then it had a negative impact on my game.

When I played against Paul, that toughness would ratchet up a notch because I wanted to be aggressive with him and hurt him. I didn't want to get him injured, it was just sibling rivalry and I wanted to show I was top dog. That's how we grew up together and it continued on in the professional game. When I carried the ball, I would try to lift my elbow if he was coming to tackle me. When it was the other way round, I'd give him a crack or come third man in. One time, as I came off the bench at the JJB Stadium, I ran to the field at the exact point we knocked the ball on and Paul dived on it. I went straight into the tackle with my knees and caught him square in the ribs. He hadn't seen who it was so started writhing and lashing out. Once he saw it was me he stopped. If that had been me, there's no way I would have stopped. Another time in 2005 David Vaealiki tackled Paul and lay all over him. Paul swung out and I thought I can't have that so jumped in and held him down. As I did that, Vaealiki absolutely hammered him. When Paul does his after-dinner speaking now, he tells people I held him down while someone gave him a hiding!

I would have loved to have played with Paul in the top flight instead of chasing him around a field for a good hammering. I got one opportunity in 2003 when I was selected for Lancashire in the Origin game against Yorkshire. My teammates Brian Carney, Paul Johnson, Terry Newton and Andy Farrell were named alongside me with Dave Hodgson our sole rep for Yorkshire. But sadly in the team run before the game Paul pulled his calf so I never got the chance. I started in the pack with Barrie McDermott and it was a fantastic experience. It was brilliant mixing with the top players from other clubs, but we were shit on the night and got battered 56-6. One bright memory from it, though, is playing with Steve Prescott and that is something I am proud of. It was his last game of rugby league, though, because he broke and split his kneecap down the middle during the game.

Incidentally, Jamie Peacock refers to part of this match in his motivational speeches and uses a video clip of him running through me. I was doing a talk with him at Huddersfield recently and he looked over at me when the clip appeared. Cheers, Jamie!

It's a shame that the Origin series didn't really take off over here. I know there are a lot of games in Super League these days and I don't know how they could work around that, but it would be good for everyone if it was brought back. They could try to get it as close as possible to State of Origin in Australia by relaxing the rules a little bit on the tough stuff. Origin was struggling over there at one point, but now it is a full-blooded, nasty, horrible game and the fans love it. It would take time, but I'm sure our fans would like to watch that sort of game and the England selectors could pick part of their Elite squad from those that played.

I'm sure that, if they had stuck with it, it could have become a massive thing. As a sport, we regularly introduce new ideas or formats or systems, but too often we don't carry them through if they don't work straightaway. That's a shame because it is impossible to build with that attitude. Saints and Wigan have a great rivalry with the Yorkshire clubs such as Leeds and Castleford, so why wouldn't it work?

Not long after we got back from the Origin camp, Wigan let Raper go and appointed Mike Gregory as his replacement. We hadn't lost that many games, but expectation at the club was high. We had been knocked out of the Challenge Cup in the semifinal to Bradford and I suppose the final straw was losing at home to Widnes 22-18 at the end of July. I got on really well with Mike and we won his first game in charge 40-0 against Halifax. We then went the rest of the season unbeaten until we lost 25-12 to Bradford in the Grand Final.

I picked up a knock in the Elimination Play-off against Warrington and missed the last two games in the run up to the final. But I was fit and good to go for a night at Old Trafford. I expected to make the side because I'd been in decent form before my injury, so I lost my temper when I was selected as 18th man for the final. I stormed into Mike's office and had a massive go at him. I accused him of picking his mates rather than the team he should have chosen. I told him I was a better player than Terry O'Connor and the only reason he was in before me was because he was his mate. To his credit, Mike soaked it up and then gave it to me good style. He said I wasn't in shape and needed to be fitter. The team went on to get battered by the Bulls and, although I missed out, it gave me no satisfaction at all.

Looking back, Mike made the right call – it was his team and he answered for those decisions. I regret that argument with him, but he was honest and straight with me. It probably did me the world of good because I knew I had to knuckle down and work harder. It was a blow, but it was softened somewhat by the fact that I had been selected for England A while I was getting ready for what I thought was a tilt at the Grand Final. I was named for the game against Australia who were touring at the time and the Euro Nations tournament with Russia, Wales and France.

The weekend before we faced the Aussies I was at my mate Chris McKinney's wedding at a hotel in Workington. At the reception I said to an old school friend, Mick Coates, that I would cause a fight against the Aussies just to wind them up. He didn't think I would so I took him up on a bet for two quid and then thought no more about it. The Aussies put out a team who were very close to their starting 17 for the Tests against Great Britain, but sadly Shane Webke didn't play. I was looking forward to facing him, but they had the likes of Joel Clinton, Danny Buderus, Petero Civoniceva and Craig Fitzgibbon to think about instead. We had a younger team who included Martin Gleeson, Rob Burrow, Danny Tickle, Sean O'Loughlin and me on the bench – all coached by John Kear. We were told there were spaces up for grabs in the GB team if we played well enough, but we knew that team was pretty well set really. Not that it mattered because we had a real good go at the Aussies and lost only 26-22. I played about half an hour in the match because I wasn't fit after missing those last three games of Wigan's season. As for the bet … I ended up scrapping with Craig Gower. I had hold of the ball in my right hand after taking it in and started throwing punches. I was hampered by the ball really and he proper leathered me and gave me a sore jaw. I texted Coatesy after the game and told him he owed me a couple of quid!

After the game we all had a couple of drinks in our hotel at Heathrow. Danny Tickle and Gareth Hock were in deep conversation about girls and all of a sudden they kicked off and went hell for leather at each other. I jumped in between them to separate them and in the end had to go and get Paul Cullen to come in and help me out. Half an hour later we were all dressed to go out and pretty tuned in and they were having a beer together! Such is the way of teammates.

The experience of being around the international team was brilliant and it made me want more. We'd come close to beating the Aussies, but we were disappointed we hadn't put one over them.

From there I was part of the England A team who swept the Euro Nations. We beat Russia 102-0 at Bradford, Wales 22-4 at Leeds and France 68-6 in the final at Warrington. In that first game I caught the ball from the kick off and carried it in, then as I hit the line, I threw a 20-metre pass to Mark Calderwood who went the length of the·field. I had done something similar in South Africa for the Under 21s and would do it against Catalans for Castleford later in my career. It was a bit of skill I honed as a kid when I wasn't allowed to score any more tries and had to set people up. It's a shame that in the modern era you're not normally allowed to do that because coaches go mental if you fuck it up. But my view is that crowds love that sort of thing and I was always taught that, if it was on, then it was worth trying wherever you are on the field. I wouldn't get picked for a side now playing like I did back then because of the 'percentages'. Coaches like robotic players and I was anything but.

Rugby league is the best sport in the world because it is

skilful, tough and anything can happen. It's not so much a spectacle as it used to be because you can't give someone a crack or do something out of the ordinary. Players have a job to do and they can't go out of their lanes. James Graham in the NRL hits the lead runner with his passing and he is a prop. But over here he can't do it for England. I used to love passing to the man at the back and then the full-back would come on to the ball from nowhere – that is great to watch! But even the NRL are beginning to take out that sort of skill although at least they have realised the game is a spectacle so have speeded things up at the ruck. We lag behind and we will have to change or we will be in trouble.

6

Up for the Cup

When I was young, every kid who was mad on rugby wanted to play in a Challenge Cup final.

The Grand Final is pretty concrete and settled in our calendar now, but growing up I wanted to walk out at Wembley playing for the most famous trophy of all. The Cup final was a big day in my house and I remember my folks bringing back a ball from Wembley in the late '80s that my brothers and I played with. It wasn't used in the game, but it came from London, from that stadium, and that was good enough to be prize possession number one in the Sculthorpe household. Those games we played in the big room on our knees were cup games in our minds and we dreamt of lifting the trophy after scoring a spectacular try or kick from the touchline.

I'd missed out on the Cup in 2002 when Saints took on Wigan because I was injured. If I had been fit, I am sure I would have got in the side and took to the field at Murrayfield. It was hard missing out on a big day and I promised myself that, if I got close again, I would try to savour every minute. I've learned that a rugby career goes by very quickly and can turn sour because of injury. In the blackness of my depression I always thought about where I had come from to be in that position. I was a rugby league player, a hard one at that, and respected at my clubs. Without that, I was nothing. It's important to savour every single moment when you're doing something you love because in a whisker it can be gone.

2004 was a special year for me at Wigan. I'd had a quality 2003, played for my country and was rewarded with a new three-year contract by the club. Chairman Maurice Lindsay was always straight with me. When I originally joined, he said he would double my deal in three years and that's exactly what he did. At the time my agent, Andy Clarke, was speaking to Saints about a potential move, but once Wigan offered me an extension, I signed on the spot. I would have loved to have gone to Paul's club, but Wigan had been good to me and offered me a fair deal.

After another ridiculously tough pre-season, I played in the opening four games of the year before missing out on our Challenge Cup quarterfinal win over Wakefield. I returned in a 21-21 draw at Saints and then we won five in a row, including a 30-18 win over Warrington at Widnes to reach the Challenge Cup final at the Millennium Stadium in Wales. There was no way I was going to miss out this time and it had the added drama of being against Saints, who were captained by my brother.

We were really keen to get the game started at Cardiff, but there was plenty of drama and emotion in the lead-up. Saints' Sean Long and Martin Gleeson were being investigated for betting on their own team to lose in a 54-8 defeat at Bradford and no-one really knew when and if any ban would be handed down. I expected them to play, but it did take some of the heat off the Warriors. We were favourites and it was good that the media were talking about something else. What I couldn't avoid was the fact I would be up against Paul. We were the first brothers to play against each other in 60-odd years in a final and the number of TV and radio interviews we did was unreal. The press had our family getting together and we were filmed passing balls at our old stomping grounds in Oldham. I didn't mind because I was used to seeing him every day anyway and it did add a bit of spice to the final. I've never shied away from the fact he is my brother and we had good fun in the build-up, but it didn't affect how each of us was going to play the game. It must have been bloody hard on our parents, though. They were so proud at seeing us both play in the biggest final of all, but they were also aware that one of us would be disappointed and upset. That said, they also couldn't lose either!

We were also aware that Mike Gregory wasn't well and that added a lot of emotion to the occasion. He didn't do a lot of public appearances before the game and that was left to his assistant Denis Betts. Everyone within the club knew he was ill, but it had been kept pretty quiet. He was suffering from motor neurone disease that was believed to be caused by an infection he got from an insect bite while travelling overseas. After a while you could see it was affecting his speech and he just wasn't the same Mike. It eventually ended his life in 2007. We wanted to win the game for him and also for a number of players we knew would be retiring or leaving the club that year. Craig Smith and Adrian Lam all talked in meetings leading up to the match about what it would mean to them and they would get upset. But it was the plight of Mike that was harder. The morning of the game he made a speech. He struggled through it and was crying, too. We all joined him and in hindsight it probably drained our energy because of the sheer emotion involved. Looking back, I think we all knew it was Mike's last chance of winning the cup, too, because of his illness. We wanted to win for him, but perhaps we played with too much emotion which stifled our performance as a result.

Boarding the bus for the final we were pretty quiet. Some players had their game heads on while others just stared out of the window, lost in their own thoughts. It was pretty surreal knowing what was to come and, when we got close to the stadium, that magnified. All you could see were Wigan and Saints fans intermingling, decked in their colours. Then, as we hit the main strip into the stadium, the fans ran out onto the road and banged on the coach. As we disembarked and entered the dressing room, the tension became pretty intense. It was a cup final derby and we knew that Saints wanted revenge for the 2002 final at Murrayfield in which we had defeated them when they were massive favourites. We knew this wasn't going to be an easy game.

The atmosphere as we walked out onto the pitch is something I will never forget. It was weird. I was used to playing in front of 25,000 at the JJB Stadium, but this felt different. Yes, there were more people and it was louder, but it was a different noise. Most of the fans had horns and they were bloody loud. Walking out into that cacophony was special and, even though he was a few players in front of me, I knew Paul was enjoying it just as much as me. I thought about Mum and Dad and how proud they would be at this moment. I would have loved to have sat next to them for just five seconds watching their reaction as we came out. It was an amazing feeling coming out into sunlight and that noise, but the game was anything but enjoyable. Saints had the big-game experience and it told in the end as they won 32-16. We never really got started, but Paul tells me I was probably Wigan's best player on the day. I'm not sure about that. All I know is that we didn't perform and we weren't good enough. It was tremendous to experience such an occasion, but upsetting to finish up as losers. It was also difficult to play because of the noise; I couldn't hear the person next to me tell me what he wanted or any of the calls on the field.

After the game Mum and Dad said they would be heading home for an early night because they felt it would be unfair to me if they stayed to celebrate with Paul. I told them to go and celebrate and not to worry because I was going to have a good night anyway – and I did. In the end they had a great night with the Saints team and celebrated Paul's triumph. It was the first time he had lifted a trophy as captain of Saints and it was the right thing for them to do. As for me? I got totally shitfaced with my mates.

When we got back from Wales, Mike travelled over to the USA to start treatment for his illness. The thinking was that if they could cure the infection, they would slow down or stop the motor neurone disease. Sadly while he was over there, they discovered it was more serious and unfortunately he never came back to coach at the club. He wanted to return later in the year, but the club wouldn't let him. He eventually sued them and received compensation in an out-of-court settlement. The whole process was hard to deal with because Mike was one of us. He understood us and had been good for my game. Betts took over and while he, like Mike, knew the culture and what the club wanted, I never got on with him as much as I did with Mike. I tried to take on board all the things he said to me, but I think there was a clash of personalities. He'd been a great player for

Wigan, but he was very young and inexperienced as a head coach and seemed to find it hard to call the shots and give orders to his former teammates.

***

We wanted to kick on after the disappointment at the Millennium Stadium and we very nearly did. We reached the final eliminator in the play-offs against Leeds, but lost out 40-12. I was in and out of the team in the latter part of the season after needing shoulder surgery. I played four more games after the Challenge Cup final and was then booked in to have my rotator cuff fixed. A day before the operation we were due to play at Hull and I got a call from Betts asking if I could play. Terry O'Connor had pulled out through illness and I was his last resort. I weighed it up and thought I couldn't do any more damage so I took to the field. I had to have a few injections to numb the pain – it was my tackling shoulder – but it felt fine. We ended up drawing the game 20-20 which was a great result and I played okay. I won respect from Denis for that, but I didn't do it for him; I did it for my teammates. Fans often don't realise when you play with a bad injury and some will criticise your performance, but that's part and parcel of the game. As soon as I got myself fit, I was back in for the play-off semifinal against Saints which we won 18-12. We took on Wakefield in the next round and then got hammered at Leeds by a team who were just too quick and too strong. A sad end to an emotional year.

After the game we went out and had a really good evening hitting the pubs around Wigan. We were already tanked up and heading down an alley to get to the next pub when one of my teammates turned around to me and asked if I was 'ripping in'. I said, 'Yeah, of course' and he pulled out a small bag of drugs, crushed it in front of me and then stuck it up his nose. I took one look at what was going on and legged it; properly got on my toes. I am very anti-drugs and I could hear him in the background shouting, 'Where are you going?' It was scary being a Wigan player at times; it was ultra-professional and totally different from my previous clubs and then that was presented to me! I like getting pissed, but what's the point in taking something to sober you up so you can start again and be twice as rough the next day?

***

It was great to get out with the boys after a long season and Mad Mondays were superb. Terry Newton's family owned the Crooked Wheel in Wigan and we would go there and get blasted. People would steal shoes from each other and throw them on the fire. One time Mick Cassidy threw a dart and it stuck in Terry's head. We would also set beer mats on fire and throw them at each other. It was ruthless, there were no boundaries and we wouldn't hold back on anyone. I made some great friends at Wigan, particularly Terry Newton, Kevin Brown and Danny Tickle. Terry was a real character who would scare players on the field. He would put them off and that would mean that our other ball players could take advantage. He would also come and take the lawnmower out of my garage without asking and then help himself to a crate of beer or a bottle of wine! We were good mates so it didn't bother me, but he would always leave the garage open. I had a nice wine collection of all different kinds in there. I would buy plenty of good bottles, but preferred Blue Nun or Black Tower because they were dead fruity!

Brian Carney was another character. He would come back to pre-season two stone overweight. First session back we would do a bleep test and he would be the first one out, quickly followed by Gary Connolly. Brian would have a blow-out in the off season, but would be the fittest as the season progressed. And Gary, despite being one of the first to drop out of the fitness sessions, was immensely strong on the field. Once he got going there was no stopping him. Terry O'Connor was another great bloke who took me under his wing and, to be honest, the accolades I got on the field were down to the likes of Terry, Craig Smith and Quentin Pongia doing the donkey work. Adrian Lam was real class and laid-back. His wife really looked after Nat and made sure she wasn't left out. It was probably daunting for her to be around Wigan and Lam's missus really helped. As for Gaz Hock, he's phenomenally talented, but a fucking nutcase! Luke Robinson was a great kid and Dave Hodgson was superb for a good Mad Monday stint because he was proper daft and funny. He could stay out for three days and not bat an eyelid – an absolute machine! Martin Aspinwall was always in a world of his own. Academically he was a really clever kid, but he had no common sense whatsoever. It was like talking to a two-year-old at times. And then there was Dave Allen, or steady Dave as he was called. He didn't give a shit about anything and would turn up to pre-season so unfit. He ended up being one of my best mates!

The off-season was a time to get away and reflect on the year gone and I had some cracking trips with the boys and Nat. One time we visited some of my friends from Rochdale

– Kay and Kirk – in Palma Nova. They had a place there. We were chatting and they said that the boxer Nigel Benn was on holiday there, too. They said he was a big friend of theirs and was also a massive Wigan fan. With Dave Allen, Danny Tickle and Gaz Hock in tow we went over to meet him and had a load of pictures taken – face-offs, fists up, the works. He was DJing over there and told us his story and all the mistakes he made growing up. I was always a Chris Eubank fan as a lad and I went to watch him train for his fight with Nigel at the Midland Hotel with my mate Shaun Whitehead. I didn't like Benn at the time because I liked Chris. But hearing his story gave me a totally different opinion.

We went back to Palma Nova after we got knocked out of the Challenge Cup in 2005 and we were at Kay and Kirk's and Nigel was there again. We got chatting, but it was the end of the trip and we were getting ready to go home. Our cases were at the side of us and Nigel asked where we were going. We'd ordered a taxi, but he took us to the airport in his Porsche Carrera. It was a half-hour journey and, when we got there, he parked up and carried our suitcases in! At the airport a young kid came up to me and asked for an autograph. I was with Nigel Benn and some kid was asking for my signature. That was very strange!

***

About 10 games into the 2005 season Betts was moved aside and Ian Millward was appointed as coach. He'd been kicked out at Saints and, despite the protestations from the Wigan fans, came on board. He was as good as gold for me at first because he put me straight into the starting line-up instead of my customary place on the bench under Denis. That didn't last forever, but it felt good that he had my back. I can't say the Millward experience was great for the rest of the players, though. Some didn't take to him at all because he would not only bollock players publicly, but also show them up in training. He would go mental; it wouldn't be criticising in a good way because he would go full bore on showing you up. He had some really good ideas about how the game should be played and you could say he showed the way forward for the sport with the way Saints played under him. He was a flair coach, but sometimes it didn't work. He came in on 30 May and we beat Salford 34-20 on the road, but then we suffered two heavy losses that will always sting Wiganers. We lost 70-0 at Leeds on 18 June and a week later got hammered at Saints 75-0 in the Cup. We were total shite in both games and we have to take the blame for that, but perhaps we just weren't set up correctly. The fans called him Agent Millward because they thought he was still working for Saints – and the Saints fans said the same, too. It wasn't that his style didn't work; it was more his personality. With my off-the-cuff game it worked early on, but when you have a coach no-one likes, then it is never going to run smoothly. The players just didn't want to play for him. We had injuries, too, and had lost Andy Farrell to Saracens which was a massive thing for the club. But Millward took us from being a top side to being complete crap and he was sacked in April the following year.

That season we never hit the heights of where we should have been and finished seventh in the table. We didn't make the play-offs, but won five of our last six games to get on the fringes of a spot in the final six at least. Saints on the other hand were flying and under Kiwi Daniel Anderson looked set to scoop the lot. They had surprisingly lost to Hull in the Challenge Cup semifinal and then we had a massive say on their Grand Final chances in September. We lost the game 38-12, but it was the damage to Sean Long and Lee Gilmour that really set them back. Terry Newton was an animal on the field and, whenever something kicked off, he always seemed to be the instigator. No-one liked to play us when Terry was in the mood; he was physically intimidating. Back in 2004 he sparked the infamous Good Friday brawl that saw Paul and Faz going at it – and Faz uttering the immortal lines that didn't need a professional lip reader to work out. Being held back by our kid after trading blows he called Saints' winger Dom Feau'nati 'a fucking shithouse' after he had flown in and attacked Stephen Wild. Thing is, that all kicked off in back play because Terry was scrapping with Jon Wilkin after he had come through on him.

On that day in September 2005 you could see in Terry's eyes that he was a man on a mission and he did Longy and Gilly good style. A high tackle floored Gilmour, but his late elbow on Long was worse. We had been told to take players out, but I never expected to see that. It was the worst tackle I have seen when I have been playing. Tez hit him full in the face with his elbow, off the ball, and fractured his cheekbone. He was sorry for what he did in the days afterwards – you want to take the best players out of the game, but he admitted to me that he went too far. He tried to apologise publicly and in private, but Longy wouldn't accept it even though they were mates. Tez eventually copped a big ban, but the damage and fall-out probably ended Saints' season. Tez was such a good player and he liked being the villain. It was good to have the opposition looking at where Terry was, and some players wouldn't back a man up because they knew he might be just around the corner. He mellowed when he was at Bradford and just wasn't that sort of player any more. He seemed happier and would have plenty of banter on the field. I played against him at the Magic Weekend for Wakefield and it was great. We had a right laugh.

At the end of the season I had played 23 games, scored two tries and felt in decent form. But within a couple of weeks I was told my career at Wigan was effectively done. Millward called me from Manchester Airport to say I was no longer in his first four props and I was therefore fifth choice. I didn't believe him because I would have been behind Bryn Hargreaves and Paul Prescott and I was better than those two players. My record had shown that. But as it all sank in, it struck me that the worst thing was the fact that he hadn't bothered to bring me in to the club to tell me face to face. I thought it was a cowardly thing to do and it came at the worst fucking time, too, because I was getting married in December. I had to find myself a club to join on loan effectively and fast. In the end Andy Clarke gave me a call to say that Cas wanted me. They offered the same money I was on at Wigan – about £90,000 a year plus £80 petrol money every Monday – and I took it on the spot. It proved to be the right move because I had a brilliant year. Terry Matterson was in charge and I loved playing for him. He gave me time off for my wedding and honeymoon, too, and I can't thank him highly enough for that.

As for Millward? In my mind he will always be a man with no bottle because of the way he got rid of me.

7

An Honest Man

One of my closest mates is a chap called Roy Williams. I met him while I was playing for Rose Bridge and, although he is 18 years my senior, we have become really close. The friendship has lasted all these years and he has been there for me and also my family in the darkest of times. When I was away, ill, injured or depressed, Roy would be there for my kids. He has been best mates with my daughter Ellie throughout her life, as well as with Louie, and taken them to all my games. He was a dad to them when I couldn't be there. I don't think he missed any of my games and several times he even travelled many miles to pick me up when I'd had operations in Oswestry and London. He is a true friend.

For Roy's 50th birthday party at the Rose and Crown in Wigan, we dressed him up as Ali G and the likeness was uncanny. But two trips with him really stand out in my memory – one to Wetherby for my stag do, but firstly to Doncaster.

Wakefield had played Saints in Paul's testimonial and, as a thank-you, he gave us £1,000 for an end-of-season piss-up. About seven of us went out and we opted to go to Doncaster races. It was a good day and once the last race finished and a few pints had gone down, we decided to drive to our hotel. We came out of Doncaster at about 2.00am and Roy told me not to head up the road because he knew a short cut. After a while we ended up in Huddersfield and I knew something was wrong. I said to him: 'How many times have you been to this hotel using this short cut?' He replied: 'Never'. It was then I realised he was more pissed than I was and we were in trouble. I got to Saddleworth and thought I'm not driving any more. I pulled over, woke Roy up and he took us the rest of the way to Wigan – with our gear still back at the hotel in Doncaster. Roy had had a pretty tough evening up to that point because he'd been assaulted by Ricky Bibey in a bar. He'd had one too many to drink, turned green and headed off sharp for the toilets. I went to see if he was okay and opened the door of one of the cubicles only to see Bibey slapping his cock on Roy's head as he brought up the contents of his stomach. All Roy could do was repeat: 'No, no, Ricky, no' before embarking on another round of heaving!

Worse was to come on my stag weekend. We went to Wetherby races on a Saturday and around Leeds afterwards. We'd had a few at the Shepherd's Boy in Oldham with breakfast before setting off over the Pennines. Then several more beers at the racecourse, so by the time we got to the Ibis in Leeds our party was in pretty bad shape. Paul and Roy lay down on their beds in the hotel and didn't wake up until the next day! The rest of us went out on the town and carried on drinking. In one pub Martin Hall's back went and his belly just popped out. He couldn't breathe in so spent the whole night holding his back with his belly on show! At 3.00am Lee and I decided to rough up Paul and Roy who had been having a nice rest. I charged into Roy's room, but I must have absolutely smashed him because he spent the next four months off work with broken ribs. He reckons he hasn't been the same since! On the way home we thought he was playing up and hungover, but he must have been in agony. The coach stopped at a pub in Oldham and then went back to Wigan with only him on it. The pain didn't subside, so his wife ended up taking him to hospital. He had an x-ray, the damage was revealed and Roy was kept in. I did feel bad about that one ... for about an hour.

My wedding on 10 December 2005 was one of the best days of my life. It was at Norton Grange in Rochdale and Nat looked absolutely amazing. It was on the same day as my former Wigan teammate Sean O'Loughlin's marriage, but I was at Cas by then so we didn't have to go through the formalities of splitting up the squad to decide who went to which do! Terry Newton and Danny Tickle came with their partners, as did Wigan stalwarts George Unsworth the kitman and Keith Mills the former player, physio and past players' association manager with their wives Irene and Anne. Terry was pretty emotional at the wedding because he had been let go by Wigan for 2006 and didn't know where he would end up. I certainly understood his position, having also been released by the club, but at least I was sorted at Castleford. The day went like a dream, there were hundreds of people there – I couldn't believe how many turned up. There were friends we hadn't seen for years, lots from different rugby clubs and it was a fantastic night. It cost about £25,000 for the whole day, but it was well worth it. We went to Fuerteventura on honeymoon a couple of days later and spent a memorable time together by the pool, relaxing, eating, drinking and soaking up the winter sunshine. I think it is likely that Ellie was conceived, too, because nine months later, on 9 October 2006, she appeared in our lives.

Finding out Nat was pregnant came as a really nice surprise. We were around at Mum and Dad's for tea with Lee and Sally and Paul and Linzi. After we had eaten, Nat was telling the girls that her period was late. Linzi asked if Nat might be pregnant and it was then that she thought she might be. On the way home we stopped off for a test kit at a 24-hour pharmacy. I remember that journey very vividly as you can see! Nat did what she needed to do, picked up the test and you could see the line. It was unbelievable; one of the best feelings ever. Two more children eventually followed Ellie, but we suffered some heartache along the way. Nat had a miscarriage before we had Louie and then two more before Isla came along. They were horrendous experiences and heart-breaking for Nat. I was at Wakefield for the first one when Nat 'phoned to tell me that she had lost the baby. She'd been for a scan and everything seemed to be going well, but it wasn't to be. The second time we were going through my problems at Bradford. We were both stressed at the time over money and potentially losing the house, so maybe that brought it on. The third was tough, too, but we got there in the end.

If I'd been in Nat's shoes, I don't know how I would have coped, but she is amazingly strong and I'm so proud of her.

8

New Beginnings

It hadn't been an easy road to becoming a professional rugby league player, but it was one I enjoyed and relished. I'd been released by Leeds and Warrington, fought back to some kind of fitness to sign for Rochdale, played for England Under 21s in South Africa and then signed for one of the world's biggest rugby league clubs in Wigan. From there I gained rep honours with Lancashire and England A and played opposite my brother in a Challenge Cup final. I was proud of my achievements and, after playing 23 times in 2005, felt I was ready to kick on and make the full international set-up. So to be told over the 'phone that I was fifth-choice prop at the club where I'd not long signed an extended deal was really shit. I'd never taken anything for granted in all my life, but I felt Millward's decision was wrong and the way he told me was appalling. Thankfully I signed for a great club in Castleford and proved to everyone that I was still a good player.

When Cas came in for me I could have said 'No.' I could have told Millward I was staying at Wigan to fight for my place because I had a contract there. But I wanted to play rugby. If I had refused to go, I would have carried on getting paid, but I might never have played another game for Wigan in the remainder of my deal there which would have crippled my chances of getting another club. I didn't really want to go to Cas at first because I thought it would be a step down. In the end, like so many decisions made after some serious thought, it was the right thing to do for my career and my family. All the doubts I'd had disappeared very quickly after just a few weeks at Wheldon Road. It was a culture shock at first, though. The training facilities weren't the best and during pre-season we were scrambling around to find a field that wasn't frozen or covered in dog shit. It was totally different from what I was used to, but as soon as I played for the team I realised why so many players loved the club.

At Wheldon Road there would be 6,000 or more fans right on top of you roaring the team on. It was like playing at a full house at Wigan. When you played Leeds, Wakefield or Bradford there, the place was rammed and the atmosphere was amazing. You hear Australian players talking about the atmosphere over here compared with their massive stadiums and places such as Castleford epitomise that – where you don't need a big venue to make a big noise. Then you have the short, wide pitch that allows the Tigers to be Classy Cas, playing free-flowing, high-scoring rugby league.

Midway through pre-season I had time off to get married and go on honeymoon, returning at Christmas. I trained for a couple of days before our traditional Boxing Day trial, which I didn't play in, and then I was fully back into it. When I signed, I had a thorough medical and undertook a lot of tests to make sure I was able to do the right things. I did a lot of testing on the rowing machine and treadmill with the conditioner Tony O'Brien and did all I could to ensure I was ready for the new season. I felt fit, healthy and ready to give it a good go for my new club – and I did just that, playing pretty well in our first five games before I faced my old club Wigan. I made my debut in a heavy 42-18 loss to Hull before we were defeated by St. Helens 44-8. Then we beat Catalans 34-28 at home, got hammered at Leeds 66-14 and beat Harlequins 34-20 on the road. Terry Matterson knew what he was getting when he signed me and he let me play my own game. He got me in for what I'd done at Wigan and Rochdale and how I could play with the ball. I must have set 10 tries up with kicks that season and I was doing 70 minutes each game. He would take me off for a few minutes here and there, but saw what I could do and let me play my way.

He was also a good man-manager. As well as letting me go on honeymoon, he allowed me to be with my family when the club played away at Catalans. They'd booked a four-day trip when the fixtures had been announced. Although my thumb was in bits, the plan was to take me with the squad to keep up the bond with them while I was out of action. Nat suggested I should ask him if I could stay with her and my folks for the trip and he said that was okay. We ended up drinking Bloody Marys in Barcelona and having a superb time. We watched the game, had a good laugh with the fans and then came home. It was like I was a fan once again and superb to be part of the supporters' Catalans experience. I loved playing in Perpignan. The atmosphere is aggressive and the home fans cheer and boo at everything. They hate you for 80 minutes, but then are your best friends. It was always physical on the field, too.

Before the Catalans game I came up against the Warriors and obviously I wanted to show them what I could do. I was hitting people hard all day and flying into every tackle and, as the first half came to a close, I cracked Bryn Hargreaves on the top of his head. Straightaway I felt pain and eventually it was diagnosed as a broken and dislocated thumb. When I came off the pitch at half time, you could see my hand was in a bad away. Our physio tried to jab it to get me through the rest of the game, but the syringe filled up with blood so we knew something bad had happened. I couldn't play the second half, but the lads went on and won the game 38-18. The next day I went to hospital and it was fused and pinned. I ended up missing nine games in total, including our win on the road at Wigan, before returning for the rest of the season.

When I came back, we'd won only five games and at that point it was clear the season was going to be a struggle. There were some very talented players in the side, but we lacked direction in the halves. With all due respect to the lads we desperately needed someone to take us around the park. We had some superb forwards in Danny Nutley and Danny Ward who were class to play alongside and Andrew Henderson at hooker. Then you throw in a young Craig Huby, Willie Manu and Richard Fa'aoso and we weren't short of power upfront. In the academy Liam Watts and Joe Westerman were just waiting for their chances. We brought Danny Brough in later in the season while Brad Davis came out of retirement and they made a big difference, but perhaps it was a little late.

We beat the top teams, but struggled against those around us. We had gained a draw at Bradford in June and then beat Huddersfield the week afterwards. Our next win came against Warrington at home when Gray Viane knocked Ben Westwood on his arse with a cracking punch.

Leeds were dispatched by a drop goal in July, but we were getting to the point where we had to win every game to stay up. Effectively we knew it was going to be hard to retain our spot in Super League when we were beaten 18-0 in early August by Wakefield at home. Monty Betham got sent off in that game for Wakefield and then Ned Catic followed him. We'd been having a tough old battle all game and that broke out into a full-blown punch-up. Ned headbutted me so I hit him twice – the first an upper cut and the second split him – but he was the one given his marching orders. In the end it didn't make any difference; we played shit and got what we deserved.

We gave ourselves a bit of a shot when we beat Quins 27-12 at home in a game that saw my bulldog Molly walk out with me as a mascot. Molly must have inspired me that day because I slipped out of a tackle and set up a try with an offload to Brad Davis. He then put Adam Fletcher over in the corner to put us clear. And on the next set I kicked a 30-metre drop goal! I got man of the match and was interviewed live on Sky by Angela Powers with Molly in my arms!

Molly was a special dog and Roy helped me to get her on the understanding that he could breed her once. She had eight pups and he made about £16,000 off the back of them! Bastard. Our physio bought one because he knew it would be a good dog for him. Molly had been around training a number of times and he and the kitman would look after her when I was running around on the field. She even had a crap on the field once and 'Luppy' the kitman went ballistic! Like most clubs, kitmen are the salt of the earth. At Castleford, Luppy did pretty much everything, including maintaining the pitch. I always looked after the kitman wherever I went. They are volunteers and players couldn't do their job without them. Okay, most are pretty tight and never hand out any gear – you had to try to cajole them into giving you any new kit. Yes, it was bribery basically to get a new running top or hoody. I don't like it, though, when players talk down to the staff and sometimes the coaches would talk to them as if they were crap, too. At Wigan when we went to America on a pre-season tour, our kitman George Unsworth had to pay for his own meals alongside the rest of the backroom staff. That was disgraceful so Jerry Seu Seu and I chipped in to pay for his food and we have been very close with George ever since.

After the Quins game we travelled to Salford and got robbed blind in a 26-16 loss. We were winning at half time, but the referee had a crap game and gave all the wrong calls, which mostly went against us. That meant we had to face Wakefield at Belle Vue in a do-or-die match for the right to stay in the Super League. Catalans were given immunity from the drop that season, so whoever finished 11th from 12 would go down. We trained well in the build-up, but once we got to Belle Vue I could sense we weren't going to win. I knew John Kear was a good motivator, he could get players up for a big game such as that and you could see it from the off. They were miles more confident than we were and it showed because we lost 29-17 in what was dubbed the Battle of Belle Vue. We finished on 19 points, three behind my old club Wigan who very nearly went down. Incidentally Millward didn't last long at Wigan and was replaced a few months into the season by Brian Noble who broke the salary cap by signing Stuart Fielden from Bradford.

At the end of the game I walked around the pitch and

thanked the Cas fans for their support. I'd had a really enjoyable year, but it had ended on a sour note. The fans were brilliant, as was everyone who worked with us behind the scenes.

But worse was to come. When I got changed and headed into the bar to meet my Dad, Roy and Nat told me he had been rushed to hospital with a stroke. It had happened before the game and they didn't tell me because they knew how important the match was for me and the club. Looking back, I'm not sure if I could have played if I'd have known. I got really upset and the loss to Wakefield and subsequent relegation didn't really matter any more. I had all my gear ready for Mad Monday and the plan was to stop at Danny Nutley's, but I went to the hospital with Roy instead. We didn't know what was wrong with him until the doctors confirmed it was Bell's palsy – a condition that affects the muscles in one side of your face. We were thankful it was just that, but on the whole it was a crap ending to a good season.

***

Castleford were a superb club – a friendly, family club where it was great to spend some time with your teammates. The coaches and backroom staff were fantastic, too, and really used to look after us. In fact, I used to take chocolates in for the lady who cooked our food. But deep in my heart I knew I wasn't going be there the following season for their Championship campaign. I know how arrogant that might sound, but I felt I was Super League standard. I'd had a good season and even thought, despite the injury to my thumb, I could have played for Great Britain at the end of the year. Danny Nutley and I were outstanding and, without being big-headed, I think I should have played for my country. Perhaps the injury and missing those games stopped that chance. If I had stayed, Castleford wouldn't have been able to offer me anything like as much money in the Championship. Danny Brough did stay with them and they got promoted the following season. With hindsight I often wish I had remained at the club and been a part of their resurgence, but at the time I wanted to stay in Super League.

I had a contract for the following season with Wigan and they wanted me back, but, after what had happened in 2005, it just didn't feel right. I spoke with Richard Cramer the sport lawyer and he organised a severance package of £25,000 for me to move on. I then started to look for another club and it wasn't too long before Wakefield came in with a three-year contract on £90,000 per season. That was a good offer. London were sniffing around again, too; Brian McDermott gave me a shout and nearly tempted me, but I'd had a bad experience of living away from home and our soon-to-be-born daughter was on the way, too. If I'd have moved down there, I would have been away from both mine and Nat's families and that would have been hard with our first child.

I'd always talk through any contracts with my Dad first to get his opinion, He would always let me know what he thought and was usually correct. When we looked at the deal from Wakefield, we thought it would be much like Castleford in terms of the club and the fans, so I signed up.

It ended up being a bad decision.

9

A Mistake

There was a fair amount of upheaval in my career when I left Wigan. I was happy at Castleford and thought I'd found a new home, but their relegation to the Championship made it pretty difficult for me to stay. I would have loved to have continued my playing days with them and I think they would have wanted me, too. In the end I chose Wakefield because it is close to Castleford and I thought both clubs would be alike. The facilities would be similar and the towns were near to each other, so I thought it would be an easy fit for me at Belle Vue. John Kear and his assistant Paul Broadbent also sold the club to me. John told me what I wanted to hear. He said I provided an x-factor and my style would suit the way he wanted Wakefield to play.

I'd come across John with England A and the Under 21s and we had got on pretty well. Okay, he didn't like his players to have fun and treated us like schoolkids, but he was a good motivator and the sides I'd been in had responded to that. I also looked forward to playing alongside David Solomona and some of the other ball-handlers at the club. But as soon as I joined the Wildcats, David was sold to Bradford. I also needed an operation on my shoulder that stopped me having a good pre-season – new teammate

Adam Watene had crunched my shoulder in the Battle of Belle Vue and it needed fixing. That put me behind the rest of the lads and it took until the fourth game of the season to make my debut.

Before that, though, a more significant change in our home life occurred when Nat gave birth to Ellie. It was superb becoming a dad for the first time and I was glad I was there to see everything, too. I have so much respect for women doing that … we complain when we tear muscles or break a bone, but they have to go through that for hours. Bringing a new life into the world was a great feeling and I wanted to do everything I could for them. I'm still the same now; if anyone were to hurt my kids, I would kill them because they mean the world to me.

Nat always understood the life of a professional player and we sorted out feeds and such things fairly quickly. I also came home from training as soon as I could so I could be involved. Being part of my kids' life is so important to me, even more so after coming through my bad times. One thing I really enjoy is seeing is Ellie with Paul's kids, Evie and Lucy, in their Christmas shows. They study at the Carol Barton School of Dance in Wigan and every Christmas they put on a show that they have trained for during the year. It lasts for four nights and Ellie has just done her seventh! When she was younger, she would always be the star of the show. She would do something daft to show off such as throwing her hat on the stage, anything like that. Now she is probably one of the best dancers there and I'm not just saying that because I am her dad. Everything seems to have clicked for her. I used to say, 'You don't have to go if you don't enjoy it.' She said she did, but she always looked so serious from concentrating, so I asked her to smile and it now comes naturally to her. Isla has started there now and it's good for her, too! I would love to have more kids, but I'm a bit OCD with them and will clean up as they move from one toy to another. I can't stand mess so maybe a fourth isn't such a good idea; however, we haven't ruled it out.

While our home life was happy with our new daughter, starting at a new club with a busted shoulder was pretty difficult. I'd played the final 20 minutes of the 'Battle' with it and it had to be fixed up. When I returned to the side, it took me ages to build up my fitness because I effectively started pre-season about two months behind my teammates and, as a result, didn't produce my best form. I made my debut away at Hull FC on 4 March 2007 in a 19-6 win, but then I appeared only another 10 times after that. I was in and out of the side and that meant I never really got going. I also had problems with my thumb following the injury I'd had at Cas. They had to fit a metal cage inside. And because they didn't want to put me under anaesthetic due to my diabetes, I watched the whole operation. I couldn't feel a thing as they numbed the area with injections and I asked them to show me when the operation was nearly done. They let me look closely before they stitched up the incisions and I saw the cage inside – I was the bionic man! It was superb. As a result, my thumb is stuck at a strange angle and I can't bend it all the way back. When I got into boxing, it was difficult to hold a fist, but I seemed to find a way around it. I also broke my hand and carried on playing, but needed a carpel tunnel op on my left hand the season after.

It was about halfway through the season when I began to feel as if I'd made a mistake in joining the club. Coupled with my stop-start beginning to life at Wakefield, I didn't rate John Kear's coaching. He'd said I had the x-factor because I played off-the-cuff and did things that props didn't do. I was supposedly what they were looking for and my style was the reason he signed me. But when I started playing, he stopped me from doing that. I always offloaded in good ball situations, but I also liked to play if I was in my own 10. I backed myself, and if it was on, it was on, and I would play what I saw. It doesn't matter where you are on the field, if it is on, you give it a go, and if you fuck up, you hold up your hands and work bloody hard on the next set of six to make sure the opposition don't punish you. But all that got stopped. Training was no fun either. Every session would be long and contain a flogging by the conditioner for at least half of it because John wouldn't do a full session on his own. In my second and third seasons Paul Broadbent took most of the sessions and it was just as bad. He was a prop by trade and would be teaching Danny Brough how to kick a ball!

John was really old-school in his style and behind the times in my opinion. He was like a schoolteacher and fun was banned. Compared with Castleford, there didn't seem to be any camaraderie and many of the players would just jump straight in their cars after training and head for home.

To John's credit he was a good motivator and that is why he has been successful. In a one-off game he can get his teams fired up and you can see why he could still do a good job for England and why he's done well in the Challenge Cup, too. Week in week out, though, I found it difficult to work with him. It was like being back in the Under 9s. Our captain, Jason Demetriou, was John's eyes and ears and I felt I couldn't trust him. And there were other players who seemed to be in John's 'inner sanctum'. As a result it was very much a split camp in the year that followed.

I could have signed for London with Brian McDermott and been a long way from home, but with hindsight it would have been better than Wakefield. I could have gone back to Wigan, too, but, because of the way they'd treated me, I wasn't willing to do that. I never once thought about quitting, though. It's not in my blood. Every time I have played the game or entered the field, I have tried to do my best. No matter how much I disliked Kear, or being at Wakefield, every time I went on the field I wanted to show what I could do. If they decided not to renew my contract, then it was essential for my future career that I was in the shop window and playing good rugby. However, my mood did affect my form. I have learned with State of Mind that if you are pissed off with life and don't enjoy being around certain people, you will take those negative thoughts and troubles onto the field. That might mean your performance drops just one per cent, which might be the difference between winning, losing, gaining a contract or being selected for your country.

I was probably close to depression at the Wildcats. I had never come across it before and didn't really know the signs. Looking back, I was showing all the indicators of not being happy with my life. But I think it was more down to being pissed off with my situation at Wakefield than what was to follow at Bradford. Thankfully, players will now speak out and admit if they are feeling down. There isn't that stigma with rugby players that there used to be. If I had spoken about it at Wigan in the early 2000s, I would have got the piss taken out of me. Now that stigma has all but gone and that is why rugby league is leading the way with State of Mind and the work of others such as former player Luke Ambler who is now a mental health campaigner. I was probably down at Wakefield, but things weren't as bad as they were to become.

Another factor that led to me being fed up with the place was the facilities and the fans. The changing rooms were shit, and I mean proper shit, with no hot water or toilet seats. They were damp and musty, too. We'd train first thing in the morning until about 10.00 and then wait until 1.00pm for the next session. Why? I have no idea, but it was usual at Wakefield under John Kear. There was a small kitchen area, but that was awful, too, and you'd be sitting around for three hours while you rested to start your next session which was ridiculous. I can understand why teams wouldn't want to go there and why Wakey have such a good record at home. It's a great pitch and 'Bathy', the kitman and groundsman, does a good job keeping it right. But the stadium is falling down. I know they are working hard to move away and everyone knows they need a new stadium.

When Castleford move to their new stadium, it would make sense for the two teams to share. But people in both towns don't want that, which I find weird. Also some of the Wakefield fans are a bit odd. On the pitch I could hear only the roar and singing, but Nat would often tell me game day was awful. Some of the fans were aggressive and would swear at players' wives during the match. By comparison Cas fans were some of the best I've played under, yet a few miles away in the next town it was completely different! I also noticed some of the differences on occasions when I was leaving the stadium in my car. Rather than someone letting you go, they would block the entrance even though I was playing for their club! I can see why Nat was intimidated on the terraces, especially if they were getting abused when things weren't going right. Fans always have a right to have a pop at you when things aren't going so well as long as it doesn't stretch the boundaries.

I never really got going in 2007 and perhaps they were expecting more from a player who was supposed to be bringing something extra to the club. Not many games stand out for me, but I do remember playing Huddersfield in round 20 and causing a massive fight. In the build-up the Giants had been telling us they were going to come and bash us up. There were some bad feelings hanging over from the last time we had faced them and I decided that someone was going to get it early. The first time I took the ball in I kicked off with Darrell Griffin. Later, after I'd had a breather, I did the same and we got stuck in again. We lost the game 24-23, but it felt better to be doing one of the things I was good at.

In 2008 I played in all but three of our games, including a Challenge Cup semifinal loss to Hull FC. My form was better than the year before and that was down to being relatively fit and having a good pre-season. We were also closer as a team, especially after what happened to Adam Watene. On 13 October 2008 Adam died of a heart attack after collapsing during a gym session at Total Fitness in Wakefield. He was 31. Adam was a fit lad who didn't smoke or drink. He was a family man and left two young kids behind. He was also a good friend and my fellow prop partner in the pack. As a result, his death hit me hard. The club had meetings and that kind of stuff for a while after it happened and to his credit Kear handled it really well. He became our rep in front of the camera and in the Press and took a lot of the heat away from us.

It was tragic losing Adam and I'd been there before, having lost teammates Karl Marriott and Roy Powell at

Rochdale. Then in March 2009 Leon Walker passed away. He was part of Wakefield's Academy and was playing against Celtic Crusaders at Maesteg. We were due to play the Crusaders at Bridgend, but got a 'phone call saying he had died on the field. The game was called off straightaway and we made our way home. It was the worst bus ride ever. We were more than five hours away from home and no-one knew what to say. At his funeral we did a guard of honour for his coffin in front of hundreds of people. It was a really sad occasion, sad for the club and sad for his family. He was a lovely kid whom I'd played alongside in friendlies. Tragic.

Health and first-aid training are important and it's vital that screening continues at clubs and even cascades down the leagues. Since Danny Jones the Keighley stand-off died, focus on this issue has become huge. His widow Lizzie has done a great job in getting defibrillators out to clubs, as have Tony and Gemma Tonks at Heartbeat of Sport who are providing education, screening equipment and defibrillators.

Speaking of education, I'd been living with diabetes since I was 16, but never really spoken about it publicly. I preferred to manage it the best I could and limit its impact on my game and lifestyle as much as possible. But sometimes it did slip over into my rugby life. The morning of our game against Saints in August 2008 I'd been in hospital because of a massive hypo. I was on a drip and in a bad way. But I came through it, went to Wakefield and played against the Saints for an hour! I didn't tell the coaches because I was desperate to play. My mouth was stuck together for most of the game because it was very dry, but I played as hard as I could and no-one would have noticed the difference. Kear thought I didn't give a toss about Wakefield towards the end of my time there – well, this goes to show I did. I still don't know how I got through that game because I shouldn't have played.

During the season I also appeared on Channel 4s *Embarrassing Bodies*. Dr. Christian Jessen asked me if a young kid might do a session with me at Wakefield. The lad had type 1 diabetes and thought he couldn't play sport with it. He was also embarrassed to tell his friends. I was interviewed about my life before he came up from Birmingham and we had a great time. It was just me and the lad, passing and tackling, having a go at the crossbar challenge and running through a few physical drills. We hadn't told him about my situation; it was more about him realising he could run and play rugby with diabetes. At the end we sat down on the terrace and, before we had sandwiches, he checked his blood and gave himself an injection. I watched him finish and then, as he took his first bite of sandwich, pulled out my machine and did the same. He was gobsmacked. He asked how I could be a pro player and diabetic. I said it didn't have to hold you back because you could learn to deal with it, get your blood levels right and be whatever you wanted to be. He went home and joined his local union team. When *Embarrassing Bodies* did a follow-up show to catch up with him, he was doing really well. His mates knew about his condition and he was playing the sport he wanted to.

I would have been the same age as he was when I was diagnosed and it was nice to show the lad where I had got to despite my diabetes. Nick Scruton and Richard Horne are also type 1 and it hasn't stopped them, has it? I was proud of getting to where I had got with the condition. Some think that type 1 people shouldn't be doing strenuous sport. Well, rugby league is the most strenuous sport and I managed it.

Diabetes could have limited that kid's life. He could have stopped playing, become depressed and let it affect the way he lived, so it was nice to have played a part in the changes he made.

***

In 2009 I left Wakefield after one last run-in with Kear. I'd started the season doing my ankle ligaments at our pre-season camp in Tenerife. In our very first session I caught a ball and stepped off the side of the pitch onto a running track that was a couple of inches lower than the pitch. As my foot hit the floor, my ankle twisted and I knew immediately it was pretty serious. I could have stayed out there, but it made sense for me to go home and Kear arranged for a flight back. It would have been hard to stay and watch the lads so it was good of him to let me go. I missed the first four games of the season, but came back in a 31-18 loss at Hull KR. I then played in seven of the next nine games before we made the trip to Harlequins. We lost that game 24-17, which was pretty disappointing because we had played well, so we had a few beers on the way back up the motorway to commiserate. There was a load of beer in the fridges so we cracked open a few and kept it pretty low-key. I had about six or seven bottles and then gave the bus driver the money for them as I got off. The day afterwards I learned that Kear had imposed a booze ban following the loss and asked for me and Danny Brough to come into his office. In the meeting he accused me of not only going against his wishes, but also stealing the beer. Nothing could have been further from the truth. Broughy hadn't paid for his, but I paid for mine and called the bus driver to confirm it there and then. Broughy apologised for breaking the ban and taking the beer, but I refused because I hadn't done anything wrong and didn't know about any booze block. He suspended me for a week and then fined me a week's wages which was about £1,800. I missed the game against Huddersfield because I was in a caravan in Bridlington for four days and Wakefield lost 54-6. I did have mixed feelings about the result – a small sense of smugness – but I did also feel sorry for my teammates.

When I returned, I again sought advice from Richard Cramer and he said the club couldn't do that because there were procedures to follow. What I did know is that during pre-season in Portugal a few of the boys went on the piss and were fined £50 each. They couldn't train the next day, but I lost a week's wages for six beers on the way home from a game. I eventually got the money back, but the damage was done. Why did Kear do it? Perhaps he wanted me to leave because in a couple of weeks I had signed for Huddersfield on loan. Perhaps he wanted to send a message to the rest of the club that this sort of 'behaviour' wouldn't be tolerated. Broughy and I were two of the highest-earning players at the club. We were experienced, well-known and well liked. The message he would have sent out would have been pretty strong, even though it was unfair. Needless to say he wasn't a coach I respected.

Mick Robinson was the football manager at Castleford and we had got on pretty well during my time there. The only thing I didn't like was a deal he set up with me and a few of the lads to buy some land. Mick talked it up and we all pitched in for the purchase because it had great potential, but the farmer who was buying it on our behalf fucked off with the money! Mick took a lot of flak for that one, but to be fair it wasn't his fault. He had joined Wakey not long before my suspension and spotted I wasn't liking it at Belle Vue. He called Nathan Brown at Huddersfield, said I was looking for a move and asked how he would feel about a swap deal. It was then mentioned to Kear and he was up for it provided Michael Korkidas came the other way. The Giants agreed and that was that. I don't know if having those six beers on the coach on the way back from London resulted in my leaving Wakefield, but if they did, then they were the best beers I ever had. I hated it at Wakefield, but Huddersfield was a great experience for me.

When I was in the caravan, I did receive a call from Chris Chester who was then assistant to Justin Morgan at Hull KR. He asked if I would consider going over there and I told him to speak to Wakefield first to see if they were interested. But Huddersfield was a better fit for me and was closer to home, too.

I left a few days after Wakefield's loss to the Giants, but Browny wouldn't let me play because he said I wasn't fit enough. He gave me proper floggings in training for about three weeks until I was ready. I made my debut against Leeds on 14 June and then played a further 12 games for the Giants, including a cracker against Catalans at home. The Dragons were always a tough side to face because their forwards were bloody massive. During the game Greg Bird came in to a tackle and cleaned me out. I have never been hit as hard as that in my life and it hurt. But I didn't want to show him he had cracked me. Alongside Bird was a chap called Jason Ryles and they came after me all day. We got the win, though, 36-12 and Browny said it was my best game for the club.

The difference between the Giants and the Wildcats was massive. The backroom staff were brilliant, as were the people upstairs in the offices, and the fans were superb, too. Tracey Haughton, the Giants' administrator, really looked after me and if I needed anything, she was only too happy to help. Browny was absolutely superb as well. Okay, he beasted me when I first arrived, but he made training fun and I enjoyed it. I was training with the likes of Paul Anderson and conditioner Mark Andrews from Australia. Browny was a players' coach; he would go out and have a beer with us after a game whereas at Wakey there was always a ban so the players would just go their own ways and do it off-site somewhere. Browny also trained with his staff before we got in and it was clear he looked after himself. He'd been a cracking player in his day and you could tell he had appeared at the highest level in the NRL.

Browny understood my game and knew which players to put alongside me by analysing what I did best. If I offloaded one way and stepped off a certain foot, he would put a player who that could take advantage next to me. He could be hard at times, you knew when he was serious, but he also knew when to relax off the field … and he had a great line in disco gear! He was a trendy guy with skinny jeans, pointy shoes, large-collared shirts with a leather jacket making appearances on most match days. For an Aussie he was pretty stylish! I'm really pleased he went out on a high with Saints by winning the Grand Final in 2014.

Although I was cup-tied, the club took me to Wembley for the 2009 Challenge Cup final against Warrington and treated me like a member of the team. I got flogged in the training session the day before the game with the rest of the team and then the night before the final, Danny Kirmond – who also wasn't playing – and I went out for a meal with the coaches. That wouldn't have happened under Kear, not a chance. The lads lost the game, but we had a great night after the final and a good bus journey home, too.

Being at the Giants was superb because I was playing long minutes and probably my best rugby, too. But all good things come to an end and what turned out to be my last game for the club was against Catalans in the Preliminary semifinal. It is strange looking back on it now because it was an emotional time. I wasn't staying at the club and a number of other players were moving on, too. It also turned out to be my last game in Super League. I had spoken to Huddersfield about staying and Browny wanted me, but I got the feeling Richard Thewlis, the CEO there, wasn't over-enthused about signing me. He offered me a contract on about £50,000 which I thought was too low and had a take-it-or-leave-it attitude, so I eventually signed for Bradford.

And that was just the start.

10

Back-Breaker

Moving to Bradford was a simple choice to make. I'd finished the season on loan at Huddersfield after moving from Wakefield and my contract was done, so I needed to find a club. The Giants offered me a contract which wasn't fantastic because they were capped-up for the following season, so when the Bulls came in and gave me a three-year deal, it made sense to move on. Steve McNamara was pretty big in the game, too, and I thought Bradford would do well. Glenn Hall, Heath L'Estrange and Matt Orford were all there and were top players. Brett Kearney was also there on a big contract. As a result, they had a squad capable of challenging right at the top and it felt like the right place to be. I also liked the idea of being a home player at Odsal. I always enjoyed going there as an away player and taking in the atmosphere of that old ground. Steve sold the club to me and I was keen to get in the front row alongside Sam Burgess. It seemed a no-brainer in the end, but, very much like Solomona at Wakefield, Sam was sold and I never got the opportunity to play alongside him!

I started pre-season a little later than planned because Nat had gallstones and had to be admitted to hospital. When I did finally make it to Odsal, I wanted to hit the ground running and get ready for a new chapter with my new club. I was in decent shape, too. At Huddersfield I couldn't have been any fitter. They flogged me before I was allowed to make my debut and I played a lot of minutes in each game. I was clocking up about an hour each match and that was a lot of time for a prop in Super League.

On signing for the Bulls I spoke about my medical history to Dr. Brown and listed all the injuries I'd had. There was no medical or any checks remotely like I'd experienced at my previous clubs, but I didn't think much about it. I expected to receive a tailored pre-season programme like I'd had at every club and, when I started training, I followed what the conditioner and physio told me to do. Like any side I have played for, you don't just go telling the medical staff what you can't or won't do. In any case my contract was set out with certain conditions because of my medical history. It included an optional third year in my favour as long as I played 15 games in the first year and 15 in the second. That was because of the previous issues I'd had with injuries. So looking back now, I can't understand why they didn't construct a programme that took into account those previous injuries.

Training began on 16 November and it seemed pretty good. I hadn't been with my teammates long, but there were the beginnings of a bond there. Rugby lads are usually very accepting and the Bulls' boys were. Michael Worrincy was my training partner and I was beginning to enjoy the craic. Six days after I started pre-season I was lifting weights – doing bent-over rowing with 60kg barbells – when I felt a sharp pain in my lower back. I went home, but it got worse and the day after I told our conditioner about the pain and requested that it be entered in the accident book.

Hello world! An early photo of me with my brothers

Posing for the camera with Paul. Check out the barnets!

On holiday with Mum, Dad, Lee and Paul

Lancashire Schoolboys. Dave Highton and Jon Duffy are pictured too and both went on to play professionally

Winning a trophy with the school team

Early days at Rochdale and looking for an offload while Darren Robinson watches

Evading a tackler with the Hornets

The watch I was given by Ray Taylor at Rochdale. I loved my time there and it was difficult to leave for Wigan

The boys! The England Under 21s in South Africa. Plenty of Super League talent here – I was chosen from Rochdale

How young do I look here?
All smiles for Wigan

See ya! Paul is
left flapping as I
go past

I played with Sinny
and against him.
I got the better of
this encounter

Chris Joynt keeping the peace as I look to do battle with Stuart Jones

Playing against Paul at Knowsley Road. Saints went and won the Grand Final after this game in 2002

Lancashire Lads! The Wigan players selected for the County of Origin team in 2003

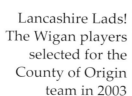

Playing for England against Wales in the 2003 European Nations Cup

Beating Warrington at Widnes to head to the 2004 Challenge Cup final

At the end of the Challenge Cup final. Celebration to deflation in 80 minutes

I had some tough battles with St Helens. Here Sean Long and I are having a bit of a disagreement

I always had an offload in my game. Sadly that doesn't happen so often in rugby league today

Congratulating my mate Terry Newton on a try, Bryn Hargreaves is on the right. He was one of the props that eventually took my spot

Cutting the cake with Natalie. Our wedding was one of the happiest days of my life

A prop who could kick. My type of rugby is redundant in the modern game

Looking to put in a tackle on my mate Terry Newton. We had a great craic when we played against each other

A publicity
photo after
signing for
Wakefield

At the birth of Ellie. Nat gave us
a beautiful daughter

Looking to offload
against Hull in the
Challenge Cup
semifinal in 2008

Walking out at Paul's testimonial game

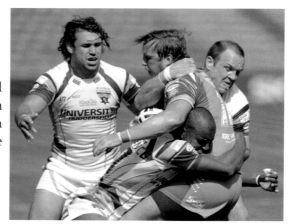

Now at the Giants and putting a big hit in on Oliver Wilkes with Scott Moore

I really enjoyed playing for Huddersfield under Nathan Brown

Playing for Widnes against York. It's hard to comprehend that a few days earlier I had been in the car park with enough drugs and alcohol to take out the entire team

My last game of rugby league. A cannonball tackle in this game ended my career and resulted in 22 operations on my knee

Taken in March 2011. I look fine here but I was hiding my depression well

Ashton Bears. I love coaching these kids

Louie showing his rugby
league skills at an early age

Ellie posing at one of her
dance shows

The State of Mind crew on one of our challenge trips

State of Mind's marquee is seen around the country

My little Isla

Delivering a State of Mind session at Cronton College in Widnes

Jimmy Gittins has become one of my closest friends; we have a lot of fun when we are working together

State of Mind is an award-winning programme and I am delighted to be involved

In my happy place presenting on mental health issues

We have a superb time at State of Mind. Spreading our message is vital but fun too. This was taken at Oxford University's Rugby League Dinner

After delivering a session at the Lancashire Sports Awards in Blackpool with paralympian Steph Slater

Our kids: Ellie,
Louie and Isla

My family are my world

A good-looking chap
spreading the word!

I was unable to train because of severe sciatic pain and was struggling to drive into the club to get checked out and undertake any kind of physio. In the end they told me to stay at home until it settled down, but it never did. It began a fucking nightmare that almost cost me my life.

The pain was horrific, but we didn't know what was causing the problem. I was struggling to move and do day-to-day things such as get dressed and play with the kids. I'd had a back injury before and was pretty positive I would come through this one, but we needed to nail down what was the exact cause. It took about a month of pain before I was sent to hospital for a MRI scan and two days before Christmas 2010 I had an epidural to see if that would stop it. It didn't do anything and I had a miserable Christmas as a result. In January it took a turn for the worse and I was struggling to walk. My dad drove me for another epidural under x-ray which was horrific. I felt every movement of the needle and screamed during the procedure. A few days later I had a consultation with Andrew King, the consultant neurosurgeon at Alexandra Hospital in Cheadle, to find out what the problem was and another MRI. I was then prescribed Oramorph, which is liquid morphine, to numb the pain. I would eventually be downing it straight from the bottle.

Nothing seemed to be working for me and I was starting to get worried. But it was when I visited Mill Lane Cemetery in Stockport to lay flowers with my folks that I realised it had gone past a simple sciatic problem. I was unable to get in any position that was comfortable in my dad's car and was in tears. Rugby league players are not supposed to show they are hurt, but there was no hiding this any more; I was in trouble. My dad 'phoned Bradford's doctor to see if

I could return to Alexandra Hospital for pain relief, but he said the hospital would not just admit for that and in any case the club's insurers wouldn't agree to it. The day after I was admitted after we contacted Mr. King directly. On 4 February I had my first operation to try to fix the problem – another discectomy and laminectomy like the one I had at Wigan. It seemed to go well, but by 18 March I was admitted to the hospital again because I couldn't walk due to the pain returning. I was diagnosed with sepsis and osteomyelitis, which is a bone infection, and prescribed teicoplanin. Eight days later I had a Hickman line fitted through my chest and into my bloodstream to feed a cocktail of antibiotics into my body to fight the infection. That line was essential because the infection was very aggressive and without it I probably wouldn't have survived.

Thankfully I didn't have to stay in hospital too long because a nursing agency was booked to come in and clean up my wounds and tubes at home. I continued to have blood tests and MRIs until I was discharged. The Hickman was taken out in June – a bloody painful operation because the skin grows around the line, so when it comes out, the only option is to cut it away at the flesh. The discomfort remained, though, and I needed a root nerve block and clindamycin to fight the infection and the pain. By 26 June I was back at the Alex on teicoplanin and ertapenem – another type of antibiotic – to fight the infection. The Hickman went back in, too, and before long the nurses would start returning to my house. Throughout this time of undergoing surgery and treatment I was still being paid by the Bulls, but not one person contacted me to see how I was. I thought this was strange because I was their player and their asset and yet they didn't really seem to care.

At the end of August the pain was still there and I was back in the Alex for a discectomy and fusion. I had a disc removed and it was replaced by wire cages and pins to stabilise the spine hopefully to stop the chronic pain. It went well and on 3 September I was discharged. I hoped that would be the end of it and that once I'd recovered I could take up my contract at the Bulls. Okay, I had been out for a while, but I still felt that I had a lot to give and I was looking forward to making my debut. But on 14 September 2010 that was taken away from me.

My agent Ron Hill called me to say he wanted to come over and tell me some news. I didn't think much about it until he knocked at my door and we chatted over a brew. He said that Bradford had terminated my contract forthwith and they wanted me to sign a compromise agreement. I couldn't believe what I was hearing. I was still recovering from six months of hell and that was me done as a Bulls player. I was disgusted at the treatment I'd received and that was made worse by the fact there had been no contact from Bradford until that very moment. I knew it wasn't right and Ron told me that, if I signed the agreement, I would have no right in law to press anything against the club. I refused to sign and a couple of days later met Simon Wilson of Hudgell Solicitors to start proceedings against the Bulls. Andy Bailey of Hattons Solicitors also helped draw up a counter-compromise agreement that would give me the right to sue if I chose to do so. Bradford eventually agreed to that and then effectively washed their hands of me. They refused to pay for any further treatment after 30 September.

All the time my mood was deteriorating and I started becoming distant from people around me. The change had begun after that first operation. I was sat in the house doing nothing. I couldn't dress or shave or move to play with the kids. Nat would ask me to get dressed and washed, but I couldn't, so I would get out of bed in the clothes I had slept in the night before. I would spend all day on the couch; I couldn't make it to the toilet or help with the housework. Nothing. This continued throughout the trips to the hospital to see the consultants which at least gave me something to do, but when I got home, it would be back on the sofa with the telly on, just staring into space. The injury was preventing me from doing anything and that made me feel that I had nothing to look forward to. We had two young kids at the time, but my head was so screwed up that I felt like there was no need for me to be alive. The kids and Nat were a blur around me, like echoes in the house. The sound was distant and life just passed me by.

I'm sure my situation wasn't helped by the drugs I was on. At times the pain was so bad I was drinking opiate painkiller direct from the bottle and taking higher and higher doses of zopiclone, a sleeping tablet. I'd been on them since my time at Wigan. I could never sleep after a game and asked the doc for a bit of help to settle down. I thought it was an ordinary thing to do because many players popped a couple after a game to help them to sleep when they were still pumped after playing. And because they helped me sleep so well I started taking them regularly. In the end I would get prescriptions from the doctor and then get my teammates to do the same and give them to me.

I ended up taking sleeping tablets every night for about 10 years and I'm sure a lot of other players have done the same. I wish I hadn't gone down that path because I have only just come off them. The sleep you get from them is unbelievable. You drop off straightaway and then get up and are good to go. I'm sure I was overdosing and then driving to training the day afterwards. It must have been affecting the way I was training, but I don't really know because I don't know what it was like training without them. It is still a major problem in rugby and a lot of players are addicted to tramadol and things like that because they think they need the stuff to get out on to the field. They take them before training and afterwards. Hopefully this is starting to fizzle out with the younger players coming through and clubs now do tests for that sort of thing.

Fighting addiction to painkillers and sleepers is hard. I remember a time when I was attempting to wean myself off the pain relief because I didn't want my life to be dictated by them. I woke up from an afternoon sleep and I couldn't breathe. It was like I was having a heart attack. My chest was tight and I couldn't force any air out. I got Nat to ring for an ambulance and, when they arrived, they could see what was going on. They gave me a paper bag to breathe into because I was having a panic attack. It was horrendous and I was throwing up out of the bedroom window into the garden while Ellie was there playing. They eventually took me to hospital and after a couple of hours I managed to regain some kind of normality.

There was another time when they let me out of hospital for a few hours to go home and see my family. It was during the regular cycle of being in and out for various checks, appointments and clean-outs. I'd been out only an hour or so before I had thumping pains travelling up my arms because of the withdrawal from the drugs. It was awful and I asked my dad to take me back because I couldn't cope.

Once I lost my job, I could feel myself slipping into a deep hole and I couldn't do anything to stop it. The painkillers, sleeping tablets, injury and contract termination compounded how I was thinking. I was getting more and more withdrawn and I started to think about ending it all. I didn't talk to anyone – rugby players didn't do that – because I didn't want people to know how useless I thought I was. I also had no idea whom I could turn to. Very quickly I went from cheeky Danny to someone I didn't recognise. I didn't want people around me, I didn't want them to see how I was and I didn't want my state of mind to infect their lives.

I'd been a very easy-going, laid-back bloke off the field and had always been very confident. I had also been a generous guy, always willing to support charity events and helping others. In fact, when I'd been at school, there had been times when I'd take other kids who couldn't afford a dinner back to our house to make them a bacon butty. But in my darkest days all that drained from me. The laughter, fun and willingness to help others disappeared and was replaced by self-obsession, introversion and a permanent sickly feeling in my stomach. I had become so depressed that I wouldn't leave the house or talk to anyone. I felt I was a failure and was ashamed that I'd lost my job and that I couldn't help those around me. And the situation got worse every day as I spiralled into the depths of my own despair.

When I first got injured at Bradford, being on the couch with my back in a mess was incredibly frustrating. We had two young children who loved jumping on their daddy and playing games, but I couldn't move, let alone do anything with them. I'm ashamed to say that over time I didn't want them around me. They became more and more of an irritation as I sank deeper into my black mood.

At the time I didn't know what was going on inside

my head and I couldn't reconcile my behaviour with being clinically depressed. It does shock me looking back at how quick it came on and it is unbelievable how events you have no control of can impact your way of thinking. Until you have been through it you don't realise. It doesn't take a massive thing in your life to bring on depression. It can be anything; little things that snowball inside your brain and the more you keep it to yourself, the more you cannot rationalise it and deal with it. Then eventually it gets to a point where you have no control over your mood and your thinking.

***

Hindsight is a wonderful thing and if I'd stayed at Huddersfield on a smaller salary, then my life would have been so much easier. The club didn't have a lot of money so maybe I should have accepted the offer instead of looking for lucrative deals elsewhere. I'm sure I would have been looked after better with the Giants and no doubt they would have tailored my training programmes better. When I signed in 2009, they knew everything about my medical history and did a risk assessment, too. And I might have finished my career only a year or so ago instead of being foisted on the scrapheap. What makes it worse is that, after signing for Bradford, I never got the chance to show the fans what I could do. They probably hate me for the action I eventually took against their club, but I wanted to play for them so much. It would have been great to turn out for that team at Odsal, but I never got the chance.

11

The Low Point

In late 2010 I forced myself to seek physiotherapy so I could try to get moving again with the hope of possibly regaining my rugby career and being able to provide for my family. It was a rare moment of clarity in my fucked-up state. I met the GB and Wigan physio Rob Harris about sorting me out and I paid him £4,000 to get me mobile. He worked out a regime for me that involved working on my core strength. The theory was the more I worked on that, the stronger my back would become. Then I could look at other things to get me into shape. Firstly he got me going for walks and they gradually became longer and longer before more physical work could begin. And it worked. I became more mobile and, although I couldn't train as hard as I wanted to do when I was playing, it didn't matter because I was out of the house and in my own bubble.

When I had been injured before, it was the club who looked after this sort of thing, but Bradford didn't want to know. As soon as the compromise was signed, they washed their hands of me. It was left to me to sort myself out and that is what I did. I started feeling better as I got fitter and it meant I could do more around the house and help my family. I would do the physio, go for a walk and then box at Paul's gym. Exercise is an anti-depressant and it was working. I also got to a point when I thought I could resume playing.

In January 2011 I met Chris Hamilton the chairman of Oldham Roughyeds and coach Tony Benson at Birch Services on the M62 to talk about possibly playing for them. They were interested in giving me a shot and I was tempted, but back then the Roughyeds paid all their players the same money – win bonuses only – and I wasn't interested. I needed to be earning regularly because the money I had got from the compromise agreement wasn't covering all my bills and the mortgage.

In the end I walked down to the Jobcentre with my dad to see if they could help and tried to claim other benefits. I remember sitting in the Jobcentre trying to get help and people were pointing at me. I could hear them saying: 'Look, that's Danny Sculthorpe', which was the worst feeling ever. I had gone from playing for Wigan and being looked up to in the community to being in the Jobcentre looking for any work that would pay me a few quid. There were some people in there genuinely looking for work, but others who were pissed, on drugs and just looking for another handout. I was embarrassed to be there and all I wanted to do was leave.

A couple of weeks later I was sitting around the kitchen table with my dad and Nat and he said we would have to sell the house. I knew he was right, but that was a horrible feeling. I loved being there; it was our home and now we would have to say goodbye to it. In the space of a fortnight all my positive thoughts were dashed and I went crashing back down into the depths of depression. The house went up for sale on 26 January and then a day later a nerve conduction test at the Alex showed I was now suffering from foot drop as a result of my discectomy and laminectomy. Not only could I not provide a roof for my family, but my body was falling apart, too!

The hospital discharged me in early February and by March I'd spoken to Denis Betts at Widnes and signed on a pay-as-you-play deal. I felt as if I could play again after all the work I had done with Rob, but it wasn't until I took to the field against Siddal in the Challenge Cup that I realised I just wasn't the same player. Because of the foot drop, every time I trained my foot would slap so I couldn't run as hard or as effectively as I wanted to. I struggled against a team far below Widnes' level, but I put it down to my first game back after a long year of surgeries.

It's hard when you realise you aren't the same player and in that first game against Siddal I realised I was miles off. Worse was to come when we travelled to Sheffield just six days later on 13 March. I was running around the pitch and really going in hard, but couldn't keep up with the pace of the game. It was passing me by and eventually I got hauled off. In the changing rooms after the game I felt like total shit and went to speak to the doctor, Jon Morgan. I told him how I felt and then asked him whether the fentanyl patches I had worn would make a difference. I'd come off the morphine for my back, but still kept using fentanyl patches to numb the pain. The patches are one of the strongest opiates you can be on for back pain and I was originally using 100mg of the stuff. I'd dropped to 75mg patches and then to 50s and was on 25s when I played at Don Valley. The doctor told me straightaway that I shouldn't be playing with them because they were a banned substance. They also explained why my energy levels were so low. Fentanyl is absorbed from the patch and as you get hotter, the more it goes in. So as I was running around, I was getting hammered with fentanyl and feeling drained. He told me I had to come off those patches immediately or I couldn't play.

I went home, slapped on a 12.5mg patch and within a week I didn't have them on at all. It was something I needed to do because if I didn't play, then there was no chance of earning any money. I spent the next three weeks not sleeping because of horrific withdrawal symptoms. My arms and legs ached all the time and, coupled with not playing, my already low mood hit rock bottom. It was clear I was addicted to the painkillers and the ease at which I fell into that trap is all too common in a sport such as rugby league. As well as the fentanyl, I was addicted to morphine and other strong painkillers. Back then, you could pretty much get anything from a doctor if you were a player and that meant addiction was an occupational hazard if they were handed out too easily. I was in chronic pain and needed to lessen it, but the power of the painkillers led to the horrific withdrawal symptoms I experienced. Thankfully in the game now club welfare officers are at least able to advise players on the risks of addiction. It is a welcome move. But not being able to play and suffering withdrawal put me into a downward spiral and I began to think there was only one way out.

Playing rugby was all I knew and, if I couldn't do that, then it was a waste of time my being here. If I couldn't provide for my family, then what was the point? I started to think about suicide every minute of every day. I would be driving along the motorway looking for bridges to hit. Could I go into that central reservation and finish it off? Could I cause a massive accident? It consumed my every thought and in the end I convinced myself there was only one way out. As my mood got lower and lower, I eventually began to get some kind of twisted focus. I hatched a plan to end my pain and misery and remove the problem that I had become for my family.

***

I pulled up at Beacon car park in Wigan and turned the engine off. There were cars all around me, but they weren't in my thoughts. On the passenger seat were all my painkillers, a bottle of gin and several cans of beer. There was enough medication there to have killed an entire rugby team, never mind one player. And I knew that if I took them, there would be no going back. I must have sat there for hours before I took the lid off the box of tablets and unscrewed the gin bottle. Fucking hell, this was it. I was going to do it and the tears were welling up in my eyes. I felt sick. I grabbed hold of the bottle, took a deep breath, held it for a while and then slowly put it back down.

To this day I don't know what flashed up in my mind to make me put those tablets down. Whether it was an image of Nat, my kids or whatever; something burrowed through the darkness into my head. The next thing I remember was returning home and putting everything back in their right and proper places. I've always been a bit OCD and wanted everything right, but I made extra care that nothing looked out of place. Maybe I was ashamed? I don't know; I just didn't want anyone to know what had happened. I didn't tell anyone where I had been; I just continued in that empty place, back on the sofa, pissed off that I hadn't seen it through.

When you make a plan like that, everything is set out and clear in your head. I was doing it for what I thought were the right reasons – I thought my family would be better off without me. But I was now in limbo, not knowing where my life would go to next. I'd looked for a way out and failed and now I was more confused than ever before. My life was contained within a seat on the sofa.

In the three weeks since I'd last played for Widnes, I'd gone through hell, but finally managed to break the fentanyl patch addiction. That meant I could play against York on 3 April and Denis called me into the team. It had been only a couple of days since I was in that car park and it showed. I played like a dickhead, trying to give someone a crack every time I went into a tackle. I got into a scrum, swinging my head on one occasion, and then ended up swinging punches the next time. After the game I got a 'phone call from the physio who was working with York and he pointed out how badly I had played and how aggressive I was. He asked if I was okay and I gave him the stock answer of 'Fine'. I couldn't tell him I was depressed; frustrated I wasn't the same player and frustrated where I was with my life. I wanted to take it out on the opposition and that is what I did. In the past giving people a hiding would have given me a boost. It would have made me feel like the player I was or might have been. But afterwards I felt totally blank. My frustrations weren't relieved at all and not even rugby could deliver me from depression.

I've spoken a number of times in this book about the stigma of not being able to speak if you are depressed and play in a macho, tough sport such as rugby league. It is difficult to admit to problems when you play a physical game. The sport is all about getting one over your opposition and finding their weakness. If anyone had known I was down, depressed or what had happened in that car park, then I would have been a target. And it's not just a sport thing. Being male means you have to be tough and not show emotion. Or at least that is a perception in society. Perhaps playing in a tough sport magnifies that. I couldn't admit I had a problem and I put up emotional barriers so I wouldn't show any weakness. And after not going through with it in the car park my life sunk to its lowest ebb. Then after playing for Widnes against Leigh four days later, my family, who had tried to cope with my moods, realised something had to be done. I'd done a good job of hiding the worst of my depression, but it couldn't be covered up any longer.

***

I was on the sofa when my Mum, Dad and Nat called me into the kitchen. They asked me to sit down, put a brew in front of me and then Nat asked what was wrong. She said they'd all noticed a big difference in me in recent weeks. They'd seen my personality change; I was watching TV day in day out, I was ignoring the kids and not talking to her. They noticed how I was acting and it had gone beyond what they had seen before. I soaked it all in and then, bang, something went off in my head. I wouldn't say it was my 'comeback' moment, but it was my moment of life. I told them how I was feeling and every thought I had in my mind; how I had let them down and my kids down; the fact I had gone from being a successful professional rugby league player to being nothing. I had gone from being on a good wage and having a good life to being on the dole and trying to make a comeback on the field when I clearly wasn't playing like I had in the past. Above all, I had lost all my dignity and confidence. We talked for hours and I lost count of the number of times we all cried; it just poured out. I told them about the suicidal thoughts, but not what happened in the car park. I wasn't ready for them to know that.

I was lucky because I have a close-knit family. I had shunned them for so long, but at last I allowed them to get near me by talking about how I felt. It didn't seem like a risk because it was my last chance anyway. And once I started talking it all just poured out. It was the beginning of my fight against depression.

Depression is a horrible illness because it is inside your head and no-one can see it. Some people will say, 'Yeah, yeah, everyone can be low, you'll snap out of it,' but it isn't that easy. If you have a broken leg, you can get it fixed, but if you are a bloke with depression, it's nothing like as simple. I told them that through no fault of my own I couldn't keep a roof over our heads or make money for my family. It was an unbelievable feeling telling them. It felt like a massive weight had been lifted from my shoulders and like I was at last seeing the light at the end of the tunnel.

We agreed I should go and see my doctor and on 20 April I did just that. I then transferred over to the doctor at Widnes because I felt more comfortable speaking to him about what was happening and he diagnosed the depression. He put me on anti-depressants of varying types and amounts. One was like a sleeping tablet, but, because I was also on zopiclone at the time, they were zoning me out. Nat later insisted I came off the sleeping tablets and I agreed to do it for her. She'd had enough of me being like a zombie and she knew I was hiding them around the house.

I did in the end, but it wasn't easy after being on them most of my career.

A side-effect from one of the anti-depressants was that it was causing me to put on weight. I was on these for a good while playing for Widnes and I ended up asking the doc whether I could come off them. He said it was okay, so I weened myself off them because of the weight gain. I have always been really conscious of my weight since I was diagnosed with diabetes and putting it back on wasn't in the plan. Ironically, while the medication and talking to my family was helping to lighten my moods, gaining weight was dragging me back down.

Only playing short periods for Widnes didn't help with my weight either. I have always got fit through playing and the situation was frustrating. Denis didn't have the confidence to play me longer even though I was in decent shape. I don't blame Denis for the way he treated me at Widnes. I was an ageing forward and nowhere near my prime, but not playing me so much didn't help me. In the end fate would shaft me once more and Denis didn't have to make another call on my fitness.

I was playing in my 11th game for the Vikings against Dewsbury when a good mate of mine, Richard Fletcher, spotted me in a tackle. I got held up while carrying the ball and he came in from the side and smashed into my knee. It wasn't intentional, but the impact snapped a bit of bone off in my knee. I had fractured my femoral condyle which was a fairly simple operation that should have seen me back playing in no time. It was fixed at the hospital in Oswestry, but I caught my usual infections and couldn't get it right or mobile enough to train. I never did play for Widnes again.

In November I had a clean-out, but within a few days it

started to weep and ooze pus. I was getting horrendous pain in my leg and my knee swelled to three times the normal size. I was admitted to Wigan Accident and Emergency and they attempted to aspirate the leg and drain the fluid. I was discharged a day later, but when I returned home, it got worse again so I was back at A and E getting it emptied once more. This was repeated twice over before they realised I'd caught a massive infection. On 15 November I was admitted to Wigan for an arthroscopy because I had staph aureus (MRSA) and septic arthritis. I was back on the morphine once again while they washed the knee out and they gave me a concoction of antibiotics to kill the infection. After that I had an emergency clean-out every three days and stayed there for a long time. I had operations on 18, 20, 23 and 28 November before one of the most serious ones on 30 November. I was admitted into the intensive care unit because the level of pain was horrific. It was so bad that, if they'd offered to amputate my leg, I would have let them. In the end they opted for a more sanguine approach and gave me a shot of ketamine. And I have to tell you it was the best feeling ever as it took the pain away. But the downside was that it made me think the nurses were coming to assassinate me and I was seeing some weird shit with the hallucinations!

I can't put into words how excruciating the pain in my knee was and it very rarely lessened throughout the multitude of operations I endured. In the end I learned how to manage and cope with it, but it was still the worst thing I think I have experienced physically. Any slight movement would send the shock waves racing around my body. Nat would take me into hospital in a wheelchair and I would be bracing myself for the tiniest of bumps on the path because I knew it would be agony. Then the thought of someone approaching to examine it would stress me out because I was so anxious about the pain I would feel. Every little touch would be absolute torture, sending stabbing pain from my knee, up through my back and front and to my head. At times I wondered if dying wouldn't be a bad thing because at least it would be over.

The operations on my knee were being undertaken by an elbow specialist and he told me he wanted to fuse my knee. That would have meant it being locked straight which would have limited my being able to walk or drive a car. I didn't want that to happen so I continued to get rehab at Oswestry. In the end I had a total of 15 operations by the time I left that hospital which included a number of different procedures such as manipulation under anaesthetic, arthroscopy, debridement and a knee capsule release.

The operations at Oswestry were managing the pain, but never really fixing the problem so I asked Paul who had fixed his knee. He suggested contacting Andrew Williams at Chelsea and Westminster Hospital. He had done Paul's knee reconstruction and the family arranged for me to head down there. He worked wonders in the end, but it was a long process. I had another capsule release at Chelsea as well as continuing my appointments at Oswestry, but in April 2014 I contracted yet another infection and had to be transferred from Wigan hospital to London. All in all I spent 102 nights in hospital and had 22 operations.

***

In December 2012, after an introduction from Emma Rosewarne at the RFL, I met Colin Bland from Sporting Chance, the charity set up by former Arsenal and England football legend Tony Adams to help sports stars with depression. Colin got me to open up about my feelings and talk about my depression. I met him twice a week for a month while I was sitting at home recovering and we talked over all the issues that had contributed to my mental state. I told him I was no use to anyone when I couldn't move off the couch because of my knee and that I couldn't do anything that was of any use to my family. He asked what was stopping me peeling spuds in preparation for the tea or folding clothes. I said 'Nothing,' so started using a Zimmer frame to get to the sink to wash up. Little things like that got me back to reality – small things that made me feel I was worth something again.

As I got stronger mentally, my meetings with Colin went from twice a week to once a week, then a fortnight, once a month and then once every three months. The counselling I went through with him saved my life. It did more for my mental state than the medication – much more. Just speaking and talking saved my life; it was that simple.

Colin was a huge support for me in my darkest days. He was there when my house was sold and regularly visited me when I was away from my family having operations in London. It was difficult mentally being in hospital for weeks at a time so far from home and, although my family visited me as much as they could, I was often alone and I used to dwell on the negative feelings and emotions. I missed Nat and the children and I was all too aware that my rugby career was now over and I was in danger of sinking back down into depression. But Colin recognised that I needed to open up and he guided me on how to handle the negative thoughts in my head. In time my mood lifted, I built up my resilience and changed from being a bloke who kept things bottled up to someone who could talk and ask for help if I needed it.

Colin also arranged for me a number of meetings with Mick Mercer from Sporting Chance. The first time he visited me I talked about what I was going through in my head, how I was feeling and my medical problems. At the second meeting we talked about things such as the news, weather and sport. And the third time we just chatted away like old mates. I realised then just talking, getting stuff off my chest and having someone whom I could discuss issues with, was what I needed. Without Colin and Mick I wouldn't be writing this now.

When I was in that car park, things were at their worst and I doubt my mental state could have deteriorated any further. The thing that started to turn everything around was the point when I spoke to my family. It completely changed from there. It was my critical moment. From that point onwards, sharing my thoughts and problems with Nat and my mum and dad slowly turned my situation around and they then helped me get the support I needed to continue my recovery.

I realise I am very lucky that my family are so close and that they were willing and able to help me. I'm lucky that they figured out that things had got really bad and sat me down and made me open up. And I'm lucky that they were able to support me and help me work through my recovery. Speaking about problems is massively underrated. When people are diagnosed with depression, anti-depressant medication is probably given out too early. When people get it, they think it will cure their depression really easily. But I think talking to my family and Colin and Mick at Sporting Chance was the thing that saved me more than the medication.

I could have not answered all their questions, but deep down inside me I was ready. They must have known I needed their help. A lot of people don't have close families and I know some people who are suffering from depression who don't have the luck I had. I had a close-knit a family to help me out. Without them I would have kept everything bottled up and I wouldn't have been here now. And I would have ruined a lot of people's lives: Nat, Ellie, Louie, Isla, Mum, Dad, Paul, Lee and the rest of the family.

Sadly, many people with depression are not as lucky as I am and don't have others to help them to work through their problems. They feel they have nowhere to turn and can't open up because of social stigma. And unfortunately it is that stigma that kills people, not the illness.

12

Money

For someone who enjoyed a decent lifestyle and also liked a really good blow-out on pay day like most people do, losing my main source of income was tough to take. I'd always been the main breadwinner in the house and my wife didn't have to go to work because I was bringing in good money. At times I was taking home £5,500 a month, but come the next pay day I had nothing left. I have never been a saver and would spend my money on my family. I preferred to give presents rather than receive, but my mantra was that life was for living. I would buy stuff for Nat and the kids and pay day would see me at the Trafford Centre in Manchester or at the Retail Park in Wigan, pushing Ellie around in her pram and buying items such as clothes and bags. In hindsight I should have saved up just in case, but I never thought my career would have ended so soon. I lived for the day and spoilt the kids.

When Bradford let me go, I struggled to make ends meet and that is what almost saw me off. I signed a redrafted compromise agreement, got a lump sum pay-out and we lived off that alongside Nat's work at Abitare, a high-end furniture store in Wigan. But because we had kids and I couldn't do anything, she worked only part-time. I'd been to the Jobcentre, too, to see what I could claim and that was horrible. Whatever money we had went into paying what we could – a complete contrast with when I would blow hundreds shopping. It is scary to think about how much we used to spend, but we can't do that now because we don't have anything like as much money coming in. If I was still on the kind of wages I was earning when I played at my height in Super League, our lives would be very comfortable.

When I signed for Widnes, I was semi-fit; it brought in appearance pay and a bonus if we won. It worked out at about £750 a game if we came out with the spoils. If I wasn't picked then, I didn't get any money and, when I was told I couldn't play because of my pain patch, it was a serious issue. I needed to play to keep food on the table and to give me a sense a dignity. Without that I was nothing. At that time I visited Wigan Citizens' Advice and they told me I could claim for industrial injuries. I was classed as 45 per cent disabled with my back injury. Now, after all the knee surgery, I am classed as 90 per cent disabled and I have a blue badge in my car. The disability benefit brought in about 80 quid a week and, when we were forced to sell the house, we were able to claim housing benefit. I could also claim sick pay. But most of this came after the house had to go up for sale. Our mortgage was about £1,250 a month and there was no way we could afford it. We ended up getting into arrears and were called in to see the bank. We told them the situation and asked if we could pay half the mortgage for a while, but the debt mounted up and we were left with no option. It was heart-breaking when dad told us we had to sell the place.

We put the house on the market at a lower price than we would have liked because we needed a quick sale. In the end, after selling the house, we still owed the bank about £15,000. I think the people who bought it knew we needed a quick sale because they were going to pay the full asking price until about two weeks before it was due to go through. They went on holiday and came back with a revised offer. We disagreed, but they wouldn't budge and we were stuck. We had to sell. It eventually went through when I was down in London having my knee done and it tipped me back into suicidal thoughts and depression. But thanks to Colin I stayed above the waterline.

I often think about what would have happened if I hadn't got injured at Widnes. I'm sure I would have finished the season with them, but I don't think I would have stayed beyond that. They got promoted and I wasn't Super League standard any more. I would have liked to have thought that I could have played out my career at Rochdale and then gone on to get my coaching badges and maybe become a coach at the Hornets. I loved the club and they always made me welcome. I would have liked to have finished there, back where I started. You just don't know where you might end up, but I wouldn't have played amateur again like some former pros. I don't know how they do that and one injury in those ranks might affect your job and livelihood, too. If I'd have been fit and playing well at Bradford, then it could have been a different story and I might have finished playing only in the last couple of years. I do miss the social side of being around the team and the banter. Rugby players can be mercilessly funny and I miss the piss-takes, the laughs and the camaraderie of a close team environment.

***

I'll talk about State of Mind later, but shortly after I got back on my feet after my operations, I decided I wanted to give something back to the organisation so I began helping them out. Paul had introduced me to them. He would talk about his mind and how having mental fitness helped him win his Man of Steel awards and played a big part in him being a better player. He would use a psychologist to get his head straight and do little routines, such as pack and unpack his bag in the same way. And it worked because he was voted the best player in 2001 and 2002. Paul took me to a training day at Hollins Park in Warrington, just to get me out of the house, and I met Dr. Phil Cooper MBE, Paul Highton, Jimmy Gittins and Martin Crompton. They were all speaking for State of Mind at the event. Paul eventually pulled out because he didn't think his story was powerful enough compared with theirs and, when I began speaking for them, mine.

After that the RFL asked if I would get involved in their disciplinary panel. I thought it was a wind-up at first given my previous history, but they wanted someone who had recently finished playing and who understood the game. My record wasn't the best so I know why players do things and if it is deliberate or reckless – a poacher turned gamekeeper, I suppose. I think players would rather have a recent player such as me on the board instead of someone who played 40 years ago and who doesn't really understand the game as it is now. I have also recently been part of the talks on betting and integrity and we've been to every professional rugby league team informing them what they can and can't do. The rules are pretty simple, but some players need reminding of their responsibilities. Basically players and officials cannot bet on any rugby league match in the country. They also cannot give out information on team selection unless their club have done it already. They can't tell anyone the squad for a game before the club have issued it because it is classed as inside information. We speak to them about the difference between spot-fixing and match-fixing, too.

One of the examples I give on the workshop relates to myself when I played at Wakefield in 2007. The players had £1,500 in our punters' club and we put it on Jamie Rooney's first goal being a penalty against Wigan at Wigan, which was our next game. It was a tight opening until eight minutes in when we won a penalty near the touchline and Rooney went for goal. John Kear was going mental on the touchline because he wanted us to roll on, but we knew that if he kicked it, we'd double our money for Mad Monday. And he did – it was worth about 1,000 pints to us which was a good couple of days at the end of the season! The point I make is that if anyone did that now they would be caught. With the technology the RFL have in their possession things, such as 'phone records, e-mails and texts, the works can all be traced back.

The guys at the RFL work really hard, but they get a lot of stick. They put a lot of time into trying to do everything they can running and developing our game. They get called the worst governing body in sport, but how can people justify that? Social media doesn't help of course and it does mean people who often don't know the facts can directly challenge those who work in the game. I responded to Sky Sports reporter Rod Studd when he said it was a disgrace that Richie Mathers had been banned for six months for disclosing inside information when he was at London. I'd spoken to Richie and others at the club three months prior to this about betting and integrity, so he knew the consequences, but went ahead and did it anyway. I bit at Rod's tweet and told him exactly what had happened. He was saying players get only six matches for taking someone's head off, but my point was he knew the consequences and got a six-month ban.

I've also received stick for being a former Wigan player on the disciplinary panel, but there rarely seems to be any mention of the fact I've also played for Rochdale, Castleford, Wakefield, Huddersfield and Widnes! I was on the panel who banned Wigan's Ben Flower for six months after that Grand Final incident with Lance Hohaia in 2014, so I can assure you there is no favouritism with me. I would never cheat and risk sacrificing the role. It means a lot to me to be still involved with the game and brings in money for my family. Why would I jeopardise that by making a dodgy decision just because I once played for Wigan? Sometimes I will argue a charge if I think it has been given incorrectly. I have argued in the past that something branded as 'reckless' is in fact more 'careless'. The Match Review Panel will grade an incident before it comes to us, but that doesn't mean we can't disagree with the grading if we want to. And we often do. Sometimes coaches come in and talk a pile of shit trying to get their player off; then you show it to them on the video and wonder how they can argue with the facts.

I'm also working for a company called Engage Presenters who were established by Paul and Jimmy Gittins a few years ago. As a prop forward I was used to using my physical ability to be successful in the game and express myself on the field. Now I use my brain and the experiences I have had with Engage. The talks I do are in a more corporate setting and I tailor my story to each different session. I talk about controlling the controllables – worrying about the things you can control rather than the stuff you can't. It's about putting things into perspective, using positivity and how you can translate that into your business and work. I'm very much a glass half-full person and I try to get that across in my presentations.

It was a pretty strange experience when I started presenting with Engage – much like it was with State of Mind. Even though I'm quite a confident and chatty guy, I've never been one for speaking in public. I wouldn't be the player giving pre-match or half time team talks and, although I did do them, I would run a mile before having to give a TV interview unless I had Molly with me, of course. But standing in front of people and adapting my stories and experiences so that they tie in with the theme of the talk I am giving is something I have found really interesting.

I have been all over the country talking to schools, colleges and businesses and it's something I'm hoping to do more of in the future. There's certainly scope for it to increase, especially the work with schools where we talk about coping with stress which is something that, with all the exams pupils take these days, is becoming a real issue. It helps to bring money in for my family and it's also making me use my brain a lot more! I've had to reinvent myself to do it.

My work is really important to me and I take it seriously. Being out of work after my injuries made me ill, so I do not take it for granted. What would I be doing now without State of Mind and my work with the RFL? I don't know. It is scary to think about it. I did personal training for a bit when I was trying to come back with Widnes. I got my level 2 gym instructor qualifications and became a level 3 fully-qualified personal trainer. I could advise on circuit training, spin-biking, food and nutrition, but didn't take it up because of my knee injury. I don't think you can have a trainer who is unable to show you how to exercise in the gym. It cost £4,000 to complete and I haven't used it. If I hadn't picked up my knee injury, I would probably have been doing that. There is no point looking back, though, only forward.

I have started a counsellor course with the intention of becoming fully qualified and helping people in the same boat as I was. Because of my story I can relate to people who are depressed and guide them through the steps. I think I am an ideal candidate to do that because it provides a marked difference from those who might know everything academically, but haven't experienced what I have. I like helping people and I know telling my story does help to save lives. I also find talking to people helps me to feel good because I know I am helping them. It is like a win-win therapy.

***

In 2015 I finally got a settlement from Bradford. I had opted to sue them because their negligence and poor treatment of me caused my life to spiral out of control. I sued the club's former holding company, Bradford Bulls Holdings Ltd., because the club had gone into administration. The claim was settled out of court by their then insurance company. I went through a no-win, no-fee solicitor to do this because I didn't have the money to pay legal fees if I lost the case. I ended up with about £40,000. To be honest I expected something like £200,000, but hearing the Bulls admitting their mistake was all I wanted.

There was a clause in my contract, as there is for all

players, that says that, if you can't train to a certain level or play within a six-month period, then the club can terminate your deal. There is a process in activating such a clause, but Bradford hadn't followed the correct procedure. They needed two different medical reports from different doctors for a start and they certainly couldn't do it over the 'phone via your agent when you hadn't heard from them for half a year. That is by the by, though, water under the bridge and it was a satisfactory end to something that took five years to sort out.

Bradford screwed me over and I hate them for what they did. But you know what? I've come through it in a new direction, with a path for the next stage of my career. Bradford have never spoken to me about that period in my life and I'm not sure I would seek out the answers from them either. I have moved on. Their then CEO, Robbie Hunter-Paul, did contact me and ask me to make it clear it was the former Bradford Bulls who did this, but I didn't take that very well. If that is the case, then do all the trophies they won earlier in Super League not matter or count as well? Of course they do, otherwise why would they have kept the Bradford Bulls name, history and colours? The club's negligence cost me my career and cost them in the courts. They admitted their mistake and settled. They admitted they were in the wrong.

Now for the next chapter.

13

It's A State Of Mind

The 'phone rang. I picked it up and it was Danny Brough giving me a call, my mate from my days at Wakefield. I was still off the scene and I thought he was giving me a shout to see what I was up to. We exchanged the usual greetings and then he asked me if I'd heard about Terry. I said, 'Terry who?' He replied with Terry Newton. Tez was one of my best mates and was always up to something or other so I jokingly said, 'What's he been up to now?' Danny replied with, 'He's hung himself.'

At the time of the call I was in Oldham buying a crate of beer because I was off to my folks for a meal. It was the day of the Championship play-offs at the Halliwell Jones Stadium in Warrington and we were having a family do. I was so shocked I just left the beer there and walked out of the shop with Danny still on the 'phone. We said goodbye and I tried to phone Terry to see if it was true. I couldn't get hold of him. I still remember that 'phone call with Danny now. It was a terrible moment and one I will never forget. Tez was one of my best mates, but couldn't open up to anyone to say what was on his mind. I was devastated. His family were, too, as were the whole rugby league community.

Whenever a tragedy happens, rugby league has a

tendency to pull itself together and act as a big family. Whether it is the community spirit within the game or the make-up of those that watch it, those in the sport always seem to support each other in times of need. From Terry's death in 2010 at just 31 years came the State of Mind charity, which established a partnership with the game. It launched in 2011 with the ethos of getting tough rugby league players to speak out when they are feeling low and trying to stop another suicide. It's just a shame it took the death of my mate for people to sit up and realise there was an issue in the sport. Just talking and someone listening is simple.

I've already mentioned several people who helped me on the road to recovery from depression, but Emma Rosewarne at the RFL certainly deserves recognition for getting me talking to a counsellor at Sporting Chance. And Colin Bland allowed me to open up and just say what was on my mind. I have since spoken for them at events and in front of all the CEOs and chairmen of the professional clubs to detail how important it is that they look after the welfare of their players. I explained to them how they need to invest in mental health and welfare because there are many players in the game who are struggling. And since Sporting Chance have been around in rugby league, more than 200 players have gone through their programmes to deal with addiction or mental health problems. Before then the RFL had a confidential helpline, but no-one had called it. To put the figures into perspective, that's 200 of about 900 professionals playing rugby league who have sought help. Rugby league is one of the toughest and most demanding of sports. Yet despite its macho reputation, many players have struggled with the emotional and mental issues and obviously kept it bottled up for too long.

I have had many Super League and Championship players and coaches and chief execs contact me asking me to speak to their players because they are worried. I do it freely, at any time of the day or night, because I don't want another Terry in the game. I know the devastation it caused his family and I know the devastation I would have caused had the outcome been different in that car park. It's just sad that it takes something like that for people to realise there is a problem and that player welfare is an important factor that must be addressed. Happy players are productive players and that is why I support what Emma is doing at the RFL by helping to push through changes in player welfare.

I miss Terry all the time and think about him a lot. I think about his kids growing up without him and then realise that might have been the situation for our children. But thankfully it wasn't and now I am helping to stop people from taking that option.

Paul introduced me to State of Mind and told Dr. Phil Cooper MBE, who was one of the founders, about my story. Phil was interested to hear what I had gone through and asked me to help. I first spoke to an audience at Rochdale Mayfield in front of the players there. I stumbled through my words, cried all the way through and finished feeling knackered and wiped out. I thought it wasn't what they wanted, but Phil said I shouldn't worry about getting upset. It was a powerful real-life story seen through the eyes of a tough rugby league professional.

It took a while, probably two years in fact, before I could talk about it without getting really upset. That wasn't the depression taking centre stage, more the thoughts of the effects it had on my family. If I was single, I probably could have spoken about what had happened to me more easily, but when I realised the stress it put on my family, it was hard. I can talk about my story now without stumbling and I often take sessions on my own. I still get upset because it still is very raw to me at times, but I think that adds to it all. I went from that stuttering session at Rochdale to speaking in front of 3,000 psychiatrists in London. I would never have thought I could have done that. When I played for Wigan, people looked up to me massively in the town. Now I've been retired some years, that's not really the case any more. But I take more joy from the results of what we do with State of Mind than I ever did from the acclaim of being a player. Playing professional rugby league was absolutely brilliant; something I always wanted to do, but it can't compare with saving someone's life.

In the last couple of years State of Mind has really taken off for me because the programme has become well-known. In the last year I have been involved in about 70 sessions at places such as schools, universities, companies, rugby league clubs, rugby union clubs, football clubs and more. Since 2011 we have delivered sessions to more than 24,000 rugby league players, coaches, fans and volunteers across the country and I've even been to Parliament to talk to the All-Party Parliamentary Rugby League Group, who consist of peers, MPs and associate members, to tell them about what State of Mind does. Our message is simple. Talk – and look after your well-being.

Some sessions really stand out for me and make me realise that the charity's role and what I am doing are really important. Although I wasn't present to witness it first-hand, we had a marquee a few years ago at a match and Phil was handing out leaflets and tips on how to stay mentally fit. He was there to offer advice and one lady brought a chap over whose son had taken his own life just two-and-a-half weeks before the game. The man was putting stuff on social media about wanting to join him. Phil spoke to him and offered lots of advice on family bereavement after a suicide. Afterwards he wandered off and Phil was worried. When he comes across people with these issues in the NHS, he has an avenue to follow it up, but on this occasion he couldn't.

After the game Phil was pulling the marquee down and the guy came back and said he had intended that this was going to be his last rugby league match. He said he planned to watch the game and then take his own life, but had changed his mind because of the information Phil had given him. A year later Phil put the marquee up at the club again and the guy came over to give him a hug. He said 'Thanks' because he was going to be a granddad. That is the power of State of Mind in what they do.

I did a talk to 1,100 kids at a school in St. Helens and after the session one of the kids went up to a teacher and said they'd heard my talk and realised something wasn't right in their life. They went home, told their mum exactly what they were going through and together they got help and support. We went back into the school two months later and one of the teachers pulled me to one side and said the student's mum had come to see her and asked her to pass on her thanks to State of Mind because she had finally got her real child back. Such stories are why we do what we do and we know there are more people out there who need help. I couldn't say how many lives we have saved, but I'm sure there are several. People who come to our sessions are hearing real-life stories of what depression can do and how you can get over it. That is powerful. Guys are realising it is actually a show of strength if you can talk about it and not a weakness.

One of the groups I also enjoy speaking to are firefighters. There is a lad called Jon Perks who played with Lee at Waterhead. He is a fireman and got us in to talk to his colleagues. They have a tough job because they are often the first people to arrive at the scene when something gruesome happens. The things those guys see must be horrific and so mental health is a massive issue. It is a very alpha male group and we try to get them to open up. We ask them to think about someone else who might be displaying symptoms of depression, but in reality we are encouraging them to think about themselves. Every second I spend with these guys is worth it.

I got asked to speak to a chap called Stuart Lannon through Andy Reid, the army veteran who lost both legs and one arm in an IED incident in Afghanistan. Stuart got an infection in his arm which went to his brain. He lost the arm and also went blind. That must be a difficult situation for him – not only losing a limb, but not being able to see his daughters grow up. I got speaking to Stuart and ended up being really close to him and taking him out for dinner. He told me he wanted to be dead, but didn't know how he was going to do it because he couldn't see. We chatted, got him help and eventually he applied for a guide dog and started to go out on his own with his stick. One thing I worked out pretty quickly is that Stuart doesn't like being pitied so we end up taking the piss out of each other. We occasionally go out for lunch with Andy and Stuart Pyke from darts and rugby league commentary fame. We are quite a combination because Andy has no legs and one arm, Pykey is pretty much deaf, Stuart is blind and has one-arm and I have a limp. Humour is what is needed sometimes when people are down. It makes a big difference when you can have a laugh and a joke and it certainly isn't one way – they can all give as much as they take.

Andy is a top bloke and I was involved in the 'Journey of Extraordinary Gentleman' in 2015 with him plus Phil, Jimmy Gittins, Mike Bradshaw and Owen Cotterell from State of Mind. Many others joined us, including Mike Burnett, Ryan Glynn and Peter Stephenson. The challenge was to hand-cycle from Hull to Manchester to deliver the ball to the Grand Final in 2015. We raised money for charity and had to pull each other through difficult times in the rain, up and down the hills across the Pennines. Jimmy was a hero in the challenge because he had broken his neck in two places when playing for Sharlston ARLFC in 2002, rendering him paralysed from the chest down. He said the event put us all on a par with him and the challenge made him realise how strong his mental state was. I was struggling with my knee, so to get to Old Trafford and watch the Wigan v Leeds Grand Final was extra special.

I have become very close to Jimmy because of State of Mind. We have spent a lot of time together and really get on. Although I have been through a lot, being with Jimmy puts things into perspective. I went through depression and a number of operations, but I came through the other side. Jimmy will never be in a good place physically and that opens my eyes, especially when I am struggling with my back or knee.

Everything Jimmy has to do physically is a toil. We did a presentation recently and had to climb 52 steps to find the room where it was taking place. That wiped him out for the rest of the day ... and we had to do another two in the same place after that as well. The demands on his body just highlight how things could have been a lot worse for me and that's why I love working with him. It's inspiring when you hear his story and you can see people in the room lift when they listen to what he has gone through.

Jimmy is a remarkable man. After his accident they told him he would never be able to sit up, wash himself or get on his own two feet. Well, he showed them in spades. He was also told he would never be able to have children and now he has two who were 'naturally conceived' as he likes to tell us. When he says that in his presentations I pipe up and say they were conceived by me. That gets a laugh and he then tells everyone we are close mates so he'll let me off.

He got into a dark place when the surgeon told him his future would be totally different. The day afterwards he asked his brother to put a pillow over his face so he could take his life because he couldn't lift it. His brother refused, stayed there and then they chatted for hours. Jimmy then decided that, if he was to survive, he had to set himself goals and he lives his life by that ethos now. The first one was to shave himself. He had a good Gillette razor taped to the back of his hand and his dad held his hand while his brother moved his elbow. They carefully put the razor around his face and gave him a shave. It may be a little thing to you or me, but being able to do something such as that was a turning-point. Mine was speaking to my family; Jimmy's was doing that shave because he was pissed off with having a cheap disposable razor pushed around his face – the only bit of his body he could feel – by a nurse. His next goal was to pick his nose and following on from that it was to wipe his arse. As far as I know he's nailed those two, but I haven't enquired too deeply!

For a guy who was told he would never be able to sit up,

he is now driving all over the country to inspire people and absolutely hammered us all on that hand-cycle ride to the Grand Final. He was also told he wouldn't be able to feed himself and believe me he has sorted that one out. He never stops eating and I have never known anyone to put it away like him. He's always on a diet!

Although I am a lot more confident and have come a long way, I do still get very emotional. I don't get depressed because I know how to manage my emotions. I could so easily have taken my own life after my playing career ended, but I didn't and I am now in a good place. It has been more than five years and, yes, of course I think about 'What ifs?' I could have ruined the lives of my kids and my wife, my parents and the rest of my family simply because I was unable to open up and talk about my emotions. As a rugby league player I would speak in front of cameras, in meetings, talk to the press and speak with the fans, but that was always about the game or having a laugh and never about what was going on in my head.

That first session at Rochdale Mayfield gave me the confidence to be me again. They knew me and knew how I played the game. If someone was in trouble on the field, I would come and defend them. For those Mayfield lads, seeing me opening up and crying meant a huge amount to them and made an impact. And the tremendous feedback I got from that first session helped with my recovery and persuaded me to do more. A few months later I spoke in front of North Wales Crusaders and broke down again. At the time I felt totally embarrassed, but again I got brilliant support from those who were there. In later sessions I could feel my heart pounding when I knew the key parts were coming up, but I soon learned that if you speak from the heart you can't go wrong. Now I don't think about it and it comes out. Sometimes I still get upset and that just depends on the venue and the people I am speaking to. In fact, it's easier to speak to an audience of 1,000 than 10 because with a small number it's very personal when you can see every face up close. My confidence has now completely come back and I'm in a brilliant place. I still hate Bradford for how they treated me, but I guess I wouldn't be doing this if it wasn't for them.

State of Mind provides me with a brilliant support network and if I have any problems I can talk to people at the organisation, particularly Phil and Malcolm Rae, the trustee chair. And at home Nat, my parents, Paul and Lee are always there for support. It is a long time since I have needed to speak, though, because these days I'm keen to be up first thing in the morning and be out and about coaching Louie, taking Ellie to her dance shows or being daft with Isla. Being well and in good mental health is about being happy with everything in your life – at home, socially and at work. If you're happy in all three, then you are in a good place.

State of Mind opened my eyes to the stigma of talking about mental health. That is why they have recruited ex-professionals to talk about their feelings. If we go to the under 19s at St. Helens and tell them that opening up to my parents and my wife saved my life, then that is a powerful story. I captained England, so if I can talk, anyone can. I was a prop forward and in that position you couldn't show you were injured or in trouble. The problems start if you take that approach into everyday life. Stigma is the killer because, if blokes feel that they can't talk, then that's when tragic things happen. My story shows these kids that they can talk, too.

Social media have also helped to break down the barriers. Mental health is spoken about a lot more on those platforms and I can see that with the retweets and messages we get at State of Mind. The more we speak, the less stigma there will be and if that saves one life it is worth it. I'm not sure if the stigma will ever go away completely, but the more we can overcome it, the less suicides there will be. The brain is an organ so there shouldn't be any issues with going to the doctor to get it fixed. It can be repaired like anything else and I am living proof of that.

Anyone who has been a professional player or played any type of team sport knows there is plenty of banter and piss-taking in the changing rooms. It all helps with team-building and strengthens the bond. But at one time it wouldn't have been possible to talk about emotional issues to your mates whereas that is now starting to change. In fact, not dealing with emotional problems inside their heads can and does affect players' performances. That can mean training becomes difficult and not getting selected for a game, which can make the problem even worse. Everything we do is driven by our brain so if that isn't fit, then a player isn't fit, no matter how fast they can run or how many weights they can lift. That was something I didn't realise when I was playing and, if I had, I'm sure I would have been a much better player. Clubs and players are now recognising that and, if State of Mind continue to do their job, then the likes of Sporting Chance won't be overrun by rugby league players. But there is still work to do and we need clubs and players to embrace this even more.

Back in my playing days if I'd told my clubs I was struggling mentally, then I doubt I would have stayed there long. And I would have been scared of not being picked or being released so I very much doubt I would have spoken about those issues. That was how it was back then, but I hope and think that clubs are becoming a lot more clued up. Do coaches understand that if someone comes and asks them for help, it is because he wants to improve himself and be as mentally fit as possible to be a top-flight player? I'd like to think so and I would hope State of Mind and the campaigns we have run open coaches' eyes to that.

It's also important that State of Mind continues to spread its message into workplaces. When I started out, we focused on rugby, but now we are starting to reach different types of organisations. Many companies are realising one of the biggest reasons for sickness absence is stress. They invite us in because they know that mentally-fit people make productive people and, as a result, a happier workplace which in turn results in a better performing company. The onus is on the individual to talk, though, and it's important you do if you have a problem. And I know from personal experience that it works!

In our work at State of Mind we prescribe 10 well-being tips. These are:

1. Talk About Your Feelings
Talking about your feelings can help you to stay in good mental health and deal with times when you feel troubled. It's part of taking charge of your well-being and doing what you can to stay healthy.

2. Eat Well
There are strong links between what we eat and how we feel – for example, caffeine and sugar can have an immediate

effect. But food can also have a long-lasting effect on your mental health.

3. Keep in Touch
Friends and family can make you feel included and cared for. They can offer different views from whatever's going on inside your own head. They can help to keep you active, keep you grounded and help you to solve practical problems.

4. Take a Break
A change of scene or a change of pace is good for your mental health. It might be a five-minute pause from cleaning your kitchen, a half-hour lunch break at work or a weekend exploring somewhere new. A few minutes can be enough to de-stress you.

5. Accept Who You Are
Some of us make people laugh, some are good at maths, others cook fantastic meals. Some of us share our lifestyle with the people who live close to us, others live very differently. We're all different.

6. Keep Active
Experts believe exercise releases chemicals in your brain that make you feel good. Regular exercise can boost your self-esteem and help you to concentrate, sleep, look and feel better. Exercise also keeps the brain and your other vital organs healthy.

7. Drink Sensibly
We often drink alcohol to change our mood. Some people

drink to deal with fear or loneliness, but the effect is only temporary.

8. Ask for Help

None of us is superhuman. We all sometimes get tired or overwhelmed by how we feel or when things go wrong. If things are getting too much for you and you feel you can't cope, ask for help.

9. Do Something You're Good At

What do you love doing? What activities can you lose yourself in? What did you love doing in the past? Enjoying yourself helps beat stress. Doing an activity you enjoy probably means you're good at it and achieving something boosts your self-esteem.

10. Care for Others

Caring for others is often an important part of keeping up relationships with people close to you. It can even bring you closer together.

14

Top Teams

One of the things I often get asked at forums and other fan events is: 'Who are the best players you've played with?'

Once you've named a couple the next question is often: 'Who are the toughest you've faced?'

I played with and against many great players in my career so I've named two teams – my 'With' and 'Against' – and even predicted the outcome if the two sides ever took to the field. Do you agree with my choices?

Played With

Full-back: Brett Hodgson

This one will probably be a bit controversial because I played with Kris Radlinski at Wigan and he was an unbelievable player who trained as hard as he played. But Brett Hodgson is a sure-fire choice because he is in the top three players I have ever played with alongside Adrian Lam and Terry Newton. Brett was absolutely class when I was at Huddersfield. He was great at training, too, but, when he was on the field, his skill level set him above the rest. He was like another half-back, but better and you could see how good he was when he moved to Warrington at the back end of his career. They certainly missed him when he left.

Wingers: Brett Dallas and Brian Carney

Brett would be in for his pure speed; he was lightning quick and could finish off anything. On the opposite wing would be Brian. He was quick, too, and could finish like Brett, but the amount of work he got through and his strength set him apart. He was a strong player and I think that is what caused his leg break in 2004. His style was to hold players off as he continued to work his way up the field. He never liked to give up the tackle and I think that contributed to three or four players falling on him and bringing about the injury. It was a bad break and it put him out for a long time.

Centres: Gary Connolly and Kevin Brown

When I played with Gary, he was coming to the end of his career, but was still an unbelievable player. He seemed to have loads of time on the ball as well as lots of strength and if anyone tried to bump him off they had no chance. He had a strong grip and would smother people and not let them go. He wouldn't miss tackles and was very skilful.

Kevin was an up-and-coming player at Wigan who wasn't scared of big names when he was making his way through. I was lucky enough to play with him at Huddersfield as well and by that time he had grown up and matured as a player. At Widnes he was so good the team revolved around him, so it was no surprise when firstly Saints and then Warrington chased his signature. He is at stand-off now and it suits him because in that position he can demonstrate how skilful he is.

Stand-off: Danny Brough

I'll confess I'm fudging this one a bit because, when I played with Danny, he was a scrum-half. But there's no way I can leave Adrian Lam out. Danny had the most amazing kicking game and his organisational skills were second to none. I also liked his doggedness. He would always take a ball in if he had to and was tough as old boots. His left foot could win you any game and it got us through a few at Wakefield. I was made up when he won the Man of Steel in 2013 because he fully deserved it, not only for what he'd done that season, but for his career, too.

Scrum-half: Adrian Lam

I watched him on the NRL Rookies show in 2016 and he hadn't changed one bit! He was the ultimate pro, but could still have a right laugh with you. The skill he showed in training was unbelievable and he took that onto the field, too. In a game you knew he had class by the amount of time he had on the ball and he transformed games as a result.

Props: Danny Sculthorpe and Danny Nutley

I was lucky enough to play with Quentin Pongia, Craig Smith and Terry O'Connor, but my prop partner would be Danny Nutley. At Castleford he would play for 80 minutes every game. He was hard as nails, would do 40 to 50 tackles a game and make 20 to 30 carries. He didn't do anything special or out of the ordinary, but did those 'one per centers' that every coach needs. He was first-class.

As for me, I always tried to play with maximum aggression and then capitalise on my athleticism and ball-handling skills when I'd intimidated the opposition.

Hooker: Terry Newton

Terry was probably the best player to have on your team because he was notorious for upsetting the opposition. You could do your thing because the other team would constantly have one eye on him and you could be confident that he always had your back. He was certainly a player you wanted alongside when things got tough. Terry could be a bit of an animal, but had a lot more skill than he was given credit for.

Second rowers: Dave Furner and Gareth Hock

Dave was a guy who had everything and was the ultimate professional. He kind of showed me the way because he got me into a group at Wigan who would do lots of extras which meant I was as fit as I could be. On the field he was hard as nails, but, much like those I've chosen, really skilful, too.

Gaz had the world at his feet, but the stuff he did off the field probably stopped him becoming an all-time great. He was pretty wild when he was a kid and would get dragged into stupid things which I think spoilt his career. He could have been one of the world's best players for sure. He is another guy who had loads of skill and was hard as nails and I know now he is at Leigh he has grown up a lot. He is a changed man, has a lovely young family and is showing what he is capable of.

Loose-forward: Andy Farrell OBE

Andy was the ultimate professional. He was the fittest in training, the strongest in the gym and led from the front. I remember when we played against Leeds and I caught him with a knee. We went in to smash Kevin Sinfield – Andy low and I high – but Sinny ducked and I ended up breaking Farrell's nose with my knee. He went off, had his nose taped up and then came back on and got the man-of-the-match. His nose was completely flat across his face and he carried on as if nothing had happened. That was him all over.

Subs.
Quentin Pongia would be one of my props on the bench and in there would also be **Willie Manu**. And from Rochdale **Darren Robinson** would get the third spot. He never played in Super League, but I loved playing alongside him. Whenever I hit the line and needed to offload, he would be there and, if I needed the ball, he would find me. He wasn't a stand-out player, but he was someone I loved playing with. Finally **Chris McKinney,** whom I played with at Rochdale and who played for Oldham Bears, would get the last spot. He was one of those players like Terry Newton who are tough as old boots. He was a second rower and, whenever you needed someone to get stuck in in defence and get on the front foot, it would be him.

Played Against

Full-back: Paul Wellens
I was lucky enough to play against Darren Lockyer, but I would choose Paul. When we were growing up, he was never a stand-out player; he was small and I suppose a late developer. But when he made his debut for the Saints, you knew what sort of player he would be and you only have to see what he has done in the game. He would always beat the first man, much like Paul Atcheson, and he would put his body on the line. He would never drop a high ball either.

161

Wingers: Lesley Vainikolo and Tevita Vaikona

Lesley was just a beast. He was a phenomenon and there isn't much more to say! He scored tries and took the hard yards and was a handful to tackle and take to the floor. He would get quick play-the-balls, set Bradford on the front foot and then that awesome foursome would come on (Joe Vagana, Stuart Fielden, Paul Anderson and Brian McDermott) with Tevita Vaikona who was big, skilful and rapid off the back of that!

Centres: Matt Gidley and Keith Senior

I thought Matt was a little bit better than Jamie Lyon actually! He was an awesome player, really skilful. Saints were lucky to have three centres in Lyon, Gidley and Martin Gleeson, all of whom could put the winger down the touchline as easily as they did.

Keith deserves to be in the team for his size and pace. I remember playing at Headingley and sometimes he would be the difference because of the breaks he would make. Every time he did there would be Danny McGuire or Rob Burrow inside him and they would finish it off. Leeds were a team of fast players and when they made a break it was odds-on they would score.

Stand-off: Lee Briers

We used to play against Lee when he was at Rainford and he was an awesome player then. At Warrington his passing and kicking game was sublime. How many of those wingers scored because of him putting in the right pass or kick? He wasn't the most professional of players and was daft as a brush when he was younger, but most of his coaches accepted that because of what he could do on the field. He was an awesome player and the amount of skill he had was frightening.

Scrum-half: Sean Long

Longy was an organiser. He would pull players around the park and knew exactly where he wanted them to be. He would kick to the corner and, because it rarely went dead, you had to work your way out of your line to defend. He was an aggressive player and hard for a scrum-half.

Props: Stuart Fielden and Paul Anderson

Stuart was another 80 minute player. He was as fit as they come, had great stamina and would run and tackle hard. He was also aggressive and was a real handful to play against. I liked facing him because it always made for a challenging game.

Paul was one of the awesome foursome at Bradford. When Joe Vagana or Fielden came off, Anderson and Brian McDermott would come on and so it was relentless. Baloo is another big guy; he was 20-odd stone, but athletic and certainly not slow. When he got up a head of steam, it was nearly impossible to stop him.

Hooker: Keiron Cunningham

Probably the hardest player I have ever played against. He would run directly at you. He would come off a quick play-the-ball and you'd just be turning in defence only to see him right in your face. He was unbelievably strong going forward and would smash you in defence, too.

Second rowers: Jamie Peacock and Willie Manu

This one was a pretty obvious call to me. Jamie played at the highest level and captained his country. He was built like Gaz Hock – being bony – and every time you tackled him you would hurt yourself. He was a top-level professional, a number one pro.

I played with Willie at Cas for a season and, when I signed for Wakefield, I spoke to John Kear and said we had to get him to the club. They tried their utmost to sign him, but he wanted to play for a bigger team so he moved to Hull. I couldn't blame him for that and he was an awesome signing for them. Willie didn't do a lot in the gym or train hard – not at Cas anyway – and he carried a lot of weight, but he was just so strong and could step. He had a devastating offload, too.

Loose-forward: Paul Sculthorpe MBE

I know what a professional Paul was. Every time we played against Saints you faced that spine of Paul, Longy, Keiron and Wello, but it was Paul who led from the front and the Saints players followed him. That spine was one of the reasons why they were so good through that era and he was at the sharp end of it. He commanded the team, kicked goals, scored tries and could do everything in the game.

Subs.

David Ferriol at Catalans was always really consistent even if he was a bit of a shithouse who would dish it out more often than not. **Sean O'Loughlin** was in the same mould as his brother-in-law, Andy Farrell, in being 100 per cent committed with loads of skill and heart.

Kevin Sinfield MBE was another captain with an unbelievable attitude. He was dedicated, professional and always seemed to kick the winning goal or drop goal in big games. He handled pressure well and never seemed to make the wrong decision. He wasn't a player who you would worry about in terms of what he could do; it was more about how he would send Leeds around the park and always put the right passes and kicks in.

Finally, Luke Dorn. He is pure lightning and at the back end of his career in England he was still scoring two or three tries a game because of his speed. When I played against him, he was at London with Mark McLinden and Thomas Leuluai and those three were brilliant together. It was always a tough game down there when they were on the pitch.

Coaches

The best coach for me was **Nathan Brown** by a country mile. This wasn't just because of his coaching – that was at a different level from everyone else – but because of the ideas he had, too. He would get players running down my right-hand side because I was a right-hand-sided offloader. I didn't realise that until he started coaching me. It was stuff like that only he could see. He was also a top man-manager. He was strict on the training ground, but would love going out and having a beer with you. I really enjoyed playing for Browny and it was a shame that Huddersfield had spent up their cap for the year I was there because I would have loved to have stayed on.

Coaching the other team would be **Terry Matterson**. He was brilliant with me. When he first came to Cas, I wasn't so sure what he would be like, but as soon as we got through the first session I knew it would be okay. He came over and said what he wanted from me and we clicked. Terry had been a skilful player, who loved playing with the ball in hand, and basically he wanted me to play my game alongside the hard stuff that was needed in my position. But he let me play pass-the-ball if it was needed and I was allowed to kick it, too. I set up five or six tries from kicks that season.

Sometimes he'd tell me after a game that I would have to rein it in a little bit and that I couldn't do everything I wanted to, but it was done in the right way because he was a top man-manager. He knew how to deal with players and would let us have a beer after a game or have fun in training. If he had been at Wigan or Saints, he would have been absolutely brilliant, but that year we struggled for half-backs before we got Danny Brough.

So who wins? I think the **Played Against** team would win, but not by much. They would take it home by four I reckon!

15

Evolution

I was looking at my 'phone recently and saw a message I sent to Dr. Phil Cooper MBE, my boss at State of Mind, at Christmas in 2016. It read: 'Thanks to you for everything you have done for me. You have given me my confidence back and I am 100 per cent back to full mental health now.'

I thought it summed up my journey perfectly from those days after being cut at Bradford to where I am now. It's taken a long time and I've been through hell, but it has been worth it.

I'm still shocked at how fast everything spiralled out of control. One minute I was the bloke everyone loved, the lad who enjoyed the banter with his mates, the cheeky bugger who loved life. The next I was on the sofa watching TV, then going to bed and repeating it day after day. I've said before it doesn't take a massive thing in your life to bring on depression. My 'moment' was serious, significant, but no different from many other people who are going through their own issues. I thought I could handle the feelings and deal with them in my own way, but before I knew where I was it had snowballed and there seemed only one way out. It got to a point where I'd had enough and that is when I nearly took my own life.

Afterwards I was pissed off I hadn't done it and felt guilty I was still on this planet. But through talking and getting stuff off my chest, through my family and the good people at Sporting Chance, I gave myself a chance at living.

And that is what I am doing now.

For a while I was still on one of the anti-depressants I was prescribed, but on the minimum 15mg dose. I took them not because of any suicidal thoughts or things I was struggling with, but more because of fear of coming off them because I didn't want to go back to that place where the thoughts of leaving my kids and family began. I didn't need the drugs, but for a while they were my emotional safety net. During the course of writing this book – itself a kind of therapy – I worked with my doctor on a seven-week, weaning-off programme. Now I don't take any at all.

Coming off the painkillers was a difficult process. After my injuries and surgeries I was taking fentanyl, OxyNorm and OxyContin and at my worst I was being hammered with ketamine to try to control the pain. I had horrendous withdrawal symptoms from them and I was also addicted to sleeping tablets which made the situation even worse. How people take stuff such as ketamine to get high I don't know. It had me hallucinating and while it helped with the pain, the side-effects were horrible.

You name it, I took it during my career. I was prescribed most types of antibiotics to deal with the infections I am prone to catching. I've been on anti-depressants and nerve relaxants such as diazepam, temazepam, amitriptyline, gabapentin, nortriptyline and pregabalin. And I've been on painkillers such as Oramorph, codeine, paracetamol, tramadol – sleepers, patches, anti-inflammatories, the works. At my worst I was necking strong opiates from the bottle. But thankfully I am on hardly any painkillers now. I am prescribed paracetamol and codeine for my back – not in big doses – and it stops the pain coming back. By keeping control of the pain it stops the injuries from flaring up and I'd rather stay on top of them than have to start back on the strong medication. I certainly don't want to be in that position again.

I take iron tablets because I am anaemic from all of the surgery I've had. I also take blood pressure medication and statins to control my cholesterol because diabetics are more at risk from heart disease and strokes.

I'm not afraid of dying, but I now want to be around to enjoy the rest of my natural life. I'm not sure what prevented me from going through with the suicide; I don't know what image popped up in my brain when I wasn't thinking straight, but I think that thoughts of my family were breaking through the turmoil in my head. And I will always be thankful for that rational moment that stopped me. I just wish I'd known what Terry Newton was thinking just before he took his own life and then I could have perhaps helped him.

I would always laugh and joke that if I got to 40 or 50 years old then I would be happy! When your time is up, it is up, but now I am in such a good place that dying is the last thing I want to do. I want to be with my wife and family and see my kids grow up, get married and have children of their own. I just don't know what I was thinking back then and how I could have even thought about going through with it. I just know it wasn't the real me sitting in that car park and that it was all because of what happened at Bradford Bulls. Their negligence, while costly in terms of my health, could have been so much worse. Their negligence nearly led to me taking my life. In a way, what Bradford did to me has made me become a better and stronger person, but I still hate them for what they put me and my family through.

Thankfully I have a strong, supportive family around me, a loving wife and three beautiful kids whom I am very proud of. Ellie was our first child and having her made our life even more special. We found out about Nat being pregnant with her when I was at Castleford so life went from being great to perfect. She was born at Wigan Hospital weighing 8lb 4oz. Ellie loves rugby league and is a massive Wigan Warriors fan. She loves dancing and has become very accomplished in the seven years she has been at Carol Barton's Dance School after starting at the age of three. She is also an excellent pupil at her regular school and that's not coming from me; that's the feedback from all her teachers who have taught her since she started at Newfold Primary in the nursery. I've every confidence she will achieve what she wants when she grows up whether that's a doctor, vet, lawyer or whatever.

When Louie was born, like Ellie it was a surprise. We didn't find out what we were having with any of them and, when he was born, I was delighted he was a boy and absolutely buzzing that we'd managed to have one of each. He was a huge, 10lb 5oz and I have no idea how Nat managed to deliver him naturally. Louie is sport-mad and can do any sport really well, from darts and golf to football and rugby. But rugby is the sport he loves most so I took him down to Ashton Bears Under 7s and he took to it like a duck to water. Whether he was running with the ball, picking kids up who ran at him or cover tackling, he shone! They were coached by Scott Hughes, Darren Hardman and Alan Molyneux at the time and now I have joined the Under

9s team and we both love it. Louie is not as good as Ellie at school; he's a typical lad who likes to mess about with his mates, but that stops when I remind him that if he doesn't focus on his school work then I'll stop his sporting activities.

Louie has an excellent PE teacher called Matt Stafford at his school who is also involved in Widnes Vikings' scholarship programme. When I can't get to games, he lets me know how Louie has done and what he needs to work on. He has brought him on a huge amount by getting him to do extra games and various after-school clubs. He's been great for Ellie, too. She isn't as sporty as Louie, but loves it because of Matt. We really appreciate what he has done for them.

Isla is lucky to have two siblings who love her so much. Louie is amazing with her while Ellie's patience sometimes wears thin, but I think that's the age gap. I have never met a kid so happy and she loves music. It's either the Sky Music channels that are on all the time or it's her favourite films: *Matilda, Home Alone, Chitty Chitty Bang Bang* or *Horrid Henry: The Movie*. Isla has recently started dancing with Ellie at Carol Barton's and adores it. If I am ever having a bad day, she always cheers me up. She also loves her rugby and can't wait for a Sunday morning so she can go and watch her big brother at Ashton Bears. Isla loves school, is very confident and has several close friends – Isla, Alyssa and Rae. She also tells me she has a boyfriend called Isaac! She was born on 28 August 2013 and was three weeks early because Nat had gestational diabetes. She is the youngest of her year instead of one of the oldest if Nat's pregnancy had gone full-term. I love her so much and always think to myself that if Nat had never had those miscarriages, then she would never have been here. Out of every negative you can always find a positive and Isla is proof!

My kids are my world and I love spending time with them. As they get older I know they will want to know more about their dad and what I did in my career. But I wouldn't let them come to a State of Mind session just yet because I couldn't speak in front of them. The only time I have spoken with one of them alongside me was at Wigan. It was a bucket collection and we were asked if we could do a talk on what we did and why I was involved. I went into the sponsors' lounge with Louie and I opened up a little more than I perhaps should have. I got upset because he was there. I don't think he fully understood what I was talking about, but it upset me to explain to the audience how at one time I would rather have been dead than be with my family. I really don't want my kids to think that could happen again.

When the appropriate time comes, I will sit down with my kids, tell them what happened and the reasons why I was thinking those things. My eldest Ellie probably knows already. She is always on the internet, typing my name and reading those stories about my time at Bradford and what happened afterwards. I have said to her that people write rubbish, but she isn't daft. I'm sure I will have to tell her the story soon and I'm sure she would understand because she is a very bright and perceptive child and so mature for her age. But I would have hated hearing that my dad would rather have been dead than with me so the timing has to be right.

I'm not ashamed of what happened. Depression is an illness like any other and I got it fixed so I shouldn't be worried about telling them. I am fully recovered now, but it's still hard to talk about as I am an emotional guy. And when I talk about what happened and get upset, it isn't me being depressed; it is just what I am like. It is something that means a lot to me.

When I was going through my counselling, a lot of my anger was directed at Bradford. Colin Bland would just listen, let me cry and afterwards I would feel so much better. Everything stayed between me and him and Nat or dad would ask how it went and what was said. I wouldn't give them any details because it was personal. Dad found that hard because he always likes to know what is going on whereas Nat found that easier to understand and asked only once. When I had my meetings with Colin, she would stay in the kitchen and she would see the difference afterwards in how much it helped me.

The bond between me and Nat is super strong. She is the rock in our relationship, the strong one, while I am the big soft arse. People would see me play and know I was a bit of a knobhead on the field who liked a scrap, but I am a big softie really. Nat is the tough one who holds us together. She looked after our kids when I couldn't do anything for them and I can't thank her enough. I don't think I could ever thank her enough and that is why I love her so much. It's amazing how we got together considering I was always pissed and trying it on. I really fancied her for ages and finally she relented and let me take her to Blackpool. I never thought from that trip we'd end up married, but here we are … and I'm still batting way above my average. We have had to move house twice since we lost our home and, although we are now settled in our own place, the upheaval of moving and the kids having to make new friends upset me. But we have now bought our own house and can put our own stamp on it rather than asking permission from landlords.

I will always stick up for my family and friends and wouldn't let anyone get the better of my kids or my wife or my mum and dad. I would die for them. It's the same with Nat's family, especially her brother Ryan whom I have become close to. I wouldn't let anyone do anything against them because of all the things they've done for me. As for my brothers? They can look after themselves and I don't need to do anything for them, but I'll be there if they need me. All my mates have been superb, too, such as 'Chicken' Les who used to supply me with chicken to sell to the boys at Widnes, Tony McGrath, Tony Greenhalgh, Paul Stevens and 'Pasty' alongside all of the other people I have spoken about. I know my depression was tough on everyone, but I'd like to think we all came out of it stronger.

My emotions still run high now, but I can control them. I have built that resilience and I can recognise a feeling and know how I can react to it. Off the field when I was playing I was probably the nicest lad you could meet. I never caused trouble when I was pissed and would do anything for anyone. On the pitch I was dirty and right on the line every time. Yes, I'd get caught for stuff when I stepped over that line, and rightly so, but if there were no dickheads in the opposition, I wouldn't have had to be so rough. There were, though, and there were often bigger players who would pick on the half-backs or the smaller, younger lads. I was never like that. I can't cope with such people, I just don't get them and it often ended up with me sorting them out. The genuinely tough players were never like that; they were just tough. Take Keiron Cunningham, he was one of the toughest I have ever played against, not because he was a scrapper, but because he was just hard. You would give him a dig and he would just laugh at you. He would then try to smash you fairly in defence and that is probably why he has so much respect in the game. Then you have the likes of Ryan Bailey who I just didn't like on the field. That said, I have respect for him now he has been able to talk about his problems and how he suffered from depression. That is massive coming from a guy who was always perceived to be a big, tough man. For him to come forward and talk about his struggles is massive for the work of State of Mind. I have come to respect him as a guy for doing that.

When I was preparing for a game, I wouldn't be serious until I crossed the line. About 10 minutes before I went to warm up I would do some boxing with the conditioner to get loose. At Wakefield I did some dumbbells to get a pump on, warm up and then just play. If I thought about the game or what was going to happen, I would get nervous and would throw up without fail. That happened from about 12-years-old, no matter how small or big the fixture. It wasn't that I was worried about the opposition and what was coming to me, more how I would play. I would worry about my performance and I would sometimes play absolutely shit because I would lose so much energy through anxiety. In the end I taught myself not to think about the game until about 10 minutes before the warm-up. I'm kidding myself here a little bit because I know I thought about the game in advance. Nat would tell me I would be snappy before a match and if anyone tried talking to me they would get it. Nat would get the brunt of it of course so I'm probably lying when I said I didn't think about it. I'm not sure I would be the same now after everything I have been through.

Other bits of my routine would see me do my bloods before a game and drink water. My bag was never packed like Paul's, all neat and tidy; it was all just thrown in the night before. That might sound messy, but I would make sure whatever I had to wear was sorted the night before so I wouldn't be messing about in the morning. I'd have a bacon butty before I played, too, and loads of water because I couldn't have any of the high sugar drinks and supplements. Eventually I started having a go at sugar-free Red Bull, though.

I'm now a very organised person and there is probably a bit of OCD there. Nat goes mad about it and, I have to admit, I used to iron my socks! She says I'm still the same and will roll her eyes if she sees me ironing a vest that will be going under my hoodie. She can't understand why I do that when no-one will see it, but the point is I know it is creased and therefore I wouldn't feel comfortable with it on. I'm a bit like my dad in that respect; he likes everything to be right. I'd rather be an hour-and-a-half early than five minutes late. I know sometimes it can't be helped, but I like to be early. You don't know what the traffic is going to be like so why not leave 20 minutes early? Nat goes mad when we are going anywhere because she likes to be last-minute. I just can't cope with that. I get dressed and get myself ready and then will pace about shouting upstairs every two minutes for her to get a move on. If I'm dressed up with a shirt and jacket on, I can't sit down because I don't like my shirt to get creased. So I wander about getting frustrated as I hear the hairdryer go on upstairs.

I also have a diary in which I write a lot of notes because I wouldn't want to let anyone down. If I didn't turn up or was double-booked or forgot something, I would feel awful. It is something I have always done, but have probably taken it a lot further since State of Mind came along. I'm on Vince Lombardi time – if you need to be at training at 6.30, you should be there by 6.10; then if something goes wrong, you have 20 minutes in the bank. I try to run my life that way. I like to be early and make sure I am prepared. I get stressed out if I'm late. I've always been like this and very regimented in a way, not like our Paul. You can tell him something, he will nod his head while looking at his 'phone and you know it has gone in one ear and straight out the other.

Okay, now the real insider stuff. The regimentation I speak about stretches into my home and it drives my family mad. When I put the shopping away, I make sure all the tins and bottles have their labels facing outwards. When I leave the house, I have to go around and make sure all the socket and light switches are off. When the kids play with their toys, I'm right behind them tidying up. My youngest Isla will get her toys out and within five minutes I have tidied them up. I hate mess! Nat goes mad at me because I machine-wash my trainers all the time. You will never see me in a mucky pair of shoes. How can people wear dirty shoes? That's not on and mine are always in the wash – at least once a fortnight.

I always wear the same clothes, too. The ones I am comfortable in will be worn for a day and then I will wash and dry them to wear the next day! That winds Nat up and she will tell me I have a wardrobe full of clothes I could wear. I will also make the bed and pretty much every time Isla will come in and jump on the duvet. She will be bouncing away and I will be tucking the duvet in and tidying around her. I can't cope with it any other way. She gets under the quilt and I'm making the bed again. I just can't relax and it's the same when we have people around for tea. I love having people around, but I can't settle until everything is cleaned up. I will make sure all the pots are done before I go to bed so they aren't there when I get up in the morning. It's just the way I am and maybe they will get used to me one day!

Louie is like me in the sense he is sport-mad and loves his rugby. When I look at him, I see me at his age – minus Paul smashing me in the face during a game of knee rugby. He went to Orrell St. James ARLFC at first to play the game and then on to Ashton Bears. Andy Ireland, the ex-Widnes, Bradford, Hull and Rochdale player, was involved at the Bears and he said I should come down, too. But he warned me that, if I did, I would be coaching at the club in six months because I'd enjoy it so much. I thought there was no chance that would happen, but guess what? It did – and it is the best thing I have ever done. I love it because it is giving something back to the younger kids. At first you could see they were in awe because I was a former player, but now they couldn't give a toss. I try to coach them into loving the game and giving them the same start I had at Oldham Juniors with Phil McLean.

The game has changed a lot since I first started playing and gone a little sterile. When I finished at Widnes, Paul Cullen said they wouldn't have kept me on because my style of play had gone. The props who could pass and had that off-the-cuff flair have been partly replaced by kick, chase, fitness, line speed and wrestle players. If you compare the Saints team of recent seasons with when Paul played, you can see the way the league has changed. Compare the current players in Super League to the likes of Paul Newlove, Kevin Iro, Tommy Martyn, Sean Long, Keiron Cunningham, Chris Joynt, Paul Wellens, Dave Fairleigh and Peter Shields. There is no comparison now and that is no disrespect to the current players. There are good players around today, but the game is different. It is faster and the collisions are bigger, but there is less skill on show. Every team seem to be playing in the same way and it has gone a bit boring as a result. You don't get the likes of Darren Britt over here any more. The players are big athletic units and maybe that is cancelling out the skill of some of them. Props look for offloads, but it's hard because three or four men are in the tackle and they clamp you. The game has evolved and the NRL is the same. It's good, but it's robotic and if you drop-off your energy in final stages, you will lose. There are things you can do to speed up the game and develop a stronger international scene, but it's all down to time and money. A bigger salary cap would help, as would less imports, the elite players spending more time together with England and bringing back a County of Origin series. Whether there is the will to do all this, only time will tell, but I'm not sure the game will ever go back to the way it was when I was growing up.

I remember going up to the Watersheddings in Oldham and seeing the likes of John Fieldhouse involved in a scrap now and again. The disciplinary rules are a lot stricter today than they used to be and I'm sure that if I was playing now I would be banned for much of the time. If I didn't give someone a crack when I played, I'd have felt like I hadn't done anything. I had to do it in every game! Now every game is watched by a review panel and every little detail is slowed down. I suppose they have to do that to ensure the big collisions are kept within the boundaries of the game. We also don't want too many bad injuries. That's fair enough, but you don't want to go too far and that is the worry because it can sanitise the sport.

I have been involved in banning players on the disciplinary panel and then once we've had sandwiches at the end, I have turned around to the other chaps and said: 'I can't believe we have just done that. Back when I played it wouldn't have been a ban!' If a player starts throwing punches now, he might be banned for three or four games. I would have been banned for sure, every week! We want to keep the game evolving, but not negatively.

I used to enjoy the banter with the refs on the pitch. I'd have a laugh with Steve Ganson and Karl Kirkpatrick. Phil Bentham is a really nice bloke, Ben Thaler is a good laugh and I got on well with Robert Hicks, too. He is a clever chap and I do a lot of work with him for off-the-field cases at the RFL. I don't mind a bad ref as long as he isn't a cheat and arrogant. Going back further, the Connolly brothers – Bob and Jon – were good, as were Tony Brown and Ian Smith. Ian is an Oldham lad and we used to go out for a beer in Lees.

When we played, if you got the refs on side and they had a little personality it would work better. Some refs realise the game is about entertainment and, if some players are slightly in the 10, as long as it is the same for both teams, they will let it go. Others will go over the top and referee by the book which I suppose is how it should be, but, let's be honest, those games aren't good to watch. Those refs never get the big games, do they? When the game is flowing, then it is more entertaining for the fans and those watching at home. I have no doubt it is a shit job to do. There are no teammates to celebrate with after a game, no cup to lift and everyone hates you. They have to look at thousands of incidents while a game is going on such as offside, passes, tackles and keeping outside the 10 and they never get thanked for it. It's never the players' fault for cocking up; it's always the refs'. And what if you make a mistake in a big game that could send a club down? Livelihoods are on the line there. It's thankless …

We're also heading into a time when concussion is becoming a big talking-point in sport all across the world. I recently received a call asking me if I would take part in a study that looked at concussion and mental health. Andy Lindley was working on this at the RFL and he knew a player who had retired because of concussion. This lad had starting taking recreational drugs because of the head knocks and they were causing him to have issues. Where that one ends up will depend on what evidence Andy can find. You only have to see what happened with Shontayne Hape who retired after more than 20 concussions brought on depression to know there could be a link. It's understandable the RFL have become over-protective of players who suffer concussions after what is happening in the NFL. I had only one or two that I know of and was never knocked out. Have they affected me? They may do in the future. I have a bad memory so you never know.

My son is going through the ranks now and I do worry about him after what I went through. But I will support him in what he wants to do and do everything I can to guide and protect him. I teach him everything I can on tackle technique and stuff like that, but I do have concerns because players such as props take hits equivalent to 30 mph car crashes in every game. That is hard on the body and many players retire at the end of their careers carrying injuries that can never properly be fixed. I'll suffer the effects of my injuries for the rest of my life and I'll need another shoulder rotator cuff fixing before too long. But that's life and the story of the sport I love. We know the risks and know the rewards. Some are unlucky I guess.

I hope I get remembered not just for what I did on the field, but also for the difference I am making now. I would like to think everyone would say I was a decent, down-to-earth lad and someone they could rely on. I don't think that is big-headed. I was brought up to respect people and I hope that comes across in my behaviour. And when my time finally comes, I hope the people at my funeral will say things such as: 'Danny Sculthorpe … decent chap, wasn't he?' And perhaps a little less seriously: 'Wasn't he good at the yard of ale?'

Back at the Beacon car park it could have gone either way. The tablets were ready and there were plenty of them with the alcohol to aid the process.

In the end I made the right decision.

Afterword

It was only recently I found out just how bad things had got for Danny and how he ended up in that car park. That might seem a strange thing to say considering I'm his wife and we've been together more than 12 years, but we've never spoken about that night.

When he was at his lowest point and told us how he was feeling, we focused on getting him the help he needed. What had brought him to that point didn't really matter, but it still came as a shock to me when he took to the stage at a State of Mind event and told everyone what had happened. It was a ladies' night in 2016 and he said beforehand that he would be on stage, but wouldn't look at me while he spoke. When he told his story, I felt immensely proud of him; proud that he had fought on and proud of him as a husband and father.

We knew something was wrong with Danny back in 2011 because everyone who knows him knows when he isn't himself. Danny is cheeky and funny, but we had seen a change with him during his recovery from the back injury that saw his contract with Bradford ripped up. His mum, dad and I had asked him what was up lots of times, but he'd say what we all say: 'I'm fine.' I knew he was down with not being able to play, but I didn't know how bad it had become. So when he told us, there was an element of relief. We knew we could do something and get him some help. And the help he received from a number of people – family, friends and professional people – mean we have the real Danny back.

I knew he wasn't right or happy, but it's difficult to ask someone directly if he is depressed. It isn't something you normally bring up in a discussion, is it? So it was hard to get him to open up about his feelings that night in the kitchen, but I'm glad we did because that was the start of his recovery

Danny is a very emotional person and he can be touchy. You can say something to him and he can take it to heart. If you say the wrong thing, no matter how trivial, he can take it the wrong way. For instance, Danny has always been really sensitive about his weight which I think comes from when it ballooned as a 16-year-old and living in Leeds. He's also very fussy and won't let me buy any clothes for him. He tends to stick to the same colours. When we met, he always wore this particular blue designer T-shirt that he never had off! But I knew he felt comfortable in it and he would wash it every night. Even now if he gets in late, he puts his stuff in the wash, waits for the machine to finish and gets them dry for the next day. He is quite domesticated and that's thanks to his mum who taught him to clean up and cook when he was younger.

I'm sure he's told you how we met so it would be interesting to see if our stories match up. I was in a relationship with one of his friends and Danny would always be round at our house because they were good mates. We split up, which meant I didn't see Danny as much, but I knew I would when I was out in Oldham on a Sunday night. I would be in town and knew if I saw Danny he would have been out all day. Every time we met he would be drunk. In one bar, Revolution, I would see him with all his rugby mates and would think to myself: 'He's had a few too many again!' I would try to avoid seeing him and would hide behind some concrete pillars in the bar.

One night I saw him and he asked to take me out again. I told him 'No,' but said he could ask me again when he wasn't drunk … but I wouldn't give him a definitive yes or no. I eventually gave in, though, and we arranged to go on a date to the cinema and then back to his house to meet his mum and dad for the first time. I remember walking in the living room and being greeted by a big, daft bulldog. Kes was her name and she was Danny's baby. I ended up staying with Danny and his parents for about six months before we bought our first house together in Oldham.

It was Danny's cheekiness that attracted me to him. Everyone who knew him found him a likeable, lovable guy and in the end I thought, 'Why not?' and gave him a chance.

I wasn't worried about being involved with a rugby league player, but it did bother me slightly when he played for Wigan. When all the lads went out after a game, I would go home and wouldn't be able to sleep until he came in. I wanted him to be safe – and knew the diabetes might affect him as well. He would down the beers and Mad Monday would see him off for days because the lager would play havoc with his blood sugar levels. Not only would he come home with someone else's top on or Brian Carney's shoes, but it would take a long time to control his blood afterwards. Now he doesn't really bother with drinking and he would rather go out for a meal instead.

Danny won't drink in the house and anyone who knows him knows he wasn't that way when he was younger! He would now rather have a brew and a biscuit at 9.00pm! Honestly. That is our routine and he is very much a routine person. When it's getting close to 9.00pm, he will say to me: 'Are you going putting your jammies on?' This is our time to chill when the children are in bed.

Being the wife of a rugby league player is probably an easy existence if your husband stays at one club. It's fair to say Danny has been at a number of clubs, but has found a home at everyone … well, nearly every one … and I have enjoyed being a part of that. When he was let go at Wigan, it came at a really difficult time because we were due to get married. We had sorted the invitations out and then he got a 'phone call from Ian Millward, who was at the airport, to say he was going out on loan. I don't think the loan bothered him; it was more the fact that Ian had called before he went off on his travels and didn't have the decency to talk to him face to face. He did well at Castleford but I know he missed the banter with the lads at Wigan. The Tigers were a great club and couldn't do enough for him – and I felt part of it, too. They even let our dog Molly be a mascot at one of the games! I know he felt he had taken a step back because he had been at the Warriors, but the move proved to be the right one.

Going from Castleford to Wakefield should have been easy, but in reality it was far from it. He didn't enjoy it there, hated the training and the booze-ban issue finished him off. We had to fight to get back the money he was fined and his heart wasn't at that club any more, but that was something he got back when he was at Huddersfield. In hindsight it would have been great for him to stay there, but the deal at Bradford was too good to turn down. What happened next you have already read, but I remember Danny's state when he couldn't sit up in the car and we had to take him to Accident and Emergency because of the pain in his back. Not one person from the Bulls telephoned or visited him throughout and then we received the news that his contract had been terminated.

Looking back, I do wonder how I got through it. Danny was in a bad place and I had to look after the house, the kids and him, too. I don't know how I kept my spirits up, but I did and never really gave it a second thought until now. He went from earning good money to practically nothing and we had to sell the house. The mortgage company could give us only so much leeway and, when his dad came over and said we'd have to sell the house, it was the worst thing we could hear. It was our first family home, but realistically there was no way around it. It was sold in 2012 and I know that was hard for Danny. I knew it wasn't his fault, but it was hard to see the 'for sale' sign go up. I had to keep okay, but some days I must have been down, too. I didn't want him to see that. I had to keep him and the kids happy and I would tell him we would get somewhere nice and start again. And you know what, we did. I don't know how we did it, but we came through it. We had to move a few times because our rented houses were sold, but now, with the help of all the family, we are settled in our own home.

There was never a point when I thought I couldn't cope. I knew I had to be there for Danny and the kids. I knew what I had to do. If I hadn't been there for him, I don't know what would have happened. I wanted him to get back to being his cheeky self. The Danny who never takes from anyone and only gives. The Danny who wants to make everyone happy.

Hearing him talking about it at that ladies' night made our story even more special and I know he loves doing what he does now. He is saving lives and I couldn't be prouder of him.

Natalie Sculthorpe, 2017

Thank You

I'd like to thank **Leeds** and **Bob Pickles** for bringing me into the professional game. While I struggled with illness and injury, it was a successful year because we won the Academy Championship. I loved being at the Campbells and they were like a second family for me, but I was very homesick and when Leeds were signing Iestyn Harris from Warrington I asked if I could go in the other direction. Thankfully the Rhinos obliged as I was struggling for fitness.

Thank you to **Warrington** for signing me and letting me move home again. I was very overweight, things didn't work out and I got released. I don't blame any of you for that and I hold no grudges.

A massive thank-you to **Rochdale Hornets, Ray** and **Barbara Taylor** and **Iain MacCorquodale** for giving me the opportunity to rebuild my career. Those years at Rochdale were my favourite time at any pro rugby club. Thank you from the bottom of my heart. I think about Ray often and miss him a lot.

To **Wigan** and **Maurice Lindsay** I owe a great deal. You gave me the chance to sign for the biggest club in the world and to live a lifelong dream.

Castleford, you gave me 12 months of great memories.

Sadly we got relegated in that famous game at Belle Vue, but if we hadn't been, then I'm sure I would have played for you for the rest of my career.

Wakefield, I thank you for letting me go on loan to Huddersfield. **The Giants** and **Nathan Brown** in particular made me enjoy my rugby again and I'm grateful for that. The chance to be coached by two great coaches in Browny and **Paul Anderson** is one I will always truly appreciate.

Bradford, I hate what you did to me and my family, putting us through the hardest years of our lives. When I got injured, you cast me to one side and left us to rot in hell. But I also thank you. Because of the depression I went through I now have a new passion and purpose in life with State of Mind. I'm using my story to inspire people and show the importance of opening up. I now have a career path built around teaching how important mental fitness is.

And to **Widnes,** even though things didn't work out, I want to thank you for giving me the opportunity to try to rebuild my career.

A big thank-you to all my **mates.** I can't mention you all individually, but you know who you are. You've been with me through all the good and bad times, supporting me in my playing career from Rochdale to England, too. And your help to get me through my darkest days has been unreal. Whenever I have needed to release my feelings, you have always been there for me. I'm really lucky to have you all as my mates.

A big thank-you also to my new teammates at **State of Mind: Malcolm Rae OBE, Dr. Phil Cooper MBE, Jimmy Gittins, Phil Veivers, Ian Knott, Ian Smith, Will Stringer, Paul Highton** and **Chris Hall**. When I got asked to join State of Mind, I was in a bad place, suffering with depression, low in confidence and physically wrecked. But, thanks to Phil and Jimmy inviting me to tell me story, my confidence grew and helped me to use the education sessions as therapy. Telling my story not only helped others, but it helped me. I have learned so much about mental health from Malcolm and Phil and they have given me the confidence to start a new career. We've travelled up and down the country and over to Northern Ireland and the Irish Republic. We speak about such an important subject, but we also have a good laugh doing it. I can honestly say that I'm in a really good place now and never been as happy. And it's mostly down to you guys. I honestly love every one of you.

Mum and **Dad**, you are the perfect parents and I can't thank you enough for everything you have ever done for me. As a kid I never needed anything. You travelled all over the country taking me to rugby matches and I am so grateful. Without your dedication to Lee, Paul and me we wouldn't be who we are today. After every game I played, you were always honest with me – whether I played well or badly – and I really did appreciate it. You were the ones I first opened up to about my depression and I'll never be able to thank you enough for saving my life. I will always try to be like you with my kids, providing support, discipline and lots and lots of love. I love you both so much and I always will.

Nat, I can't thank you enough for giving us the most important people in our lives, our three gorgeous kids. You were my rock when my depression hit, your patience was incredible and without you I doubt I would be here. You held our family together and I can't thank you enough. You are not only my wife, but also my best friend and I love you more every day. Our future is something I am really looking forward to and I've never been as happy as I am now. You've saved my life when I have had bad hypos with my diabetes and, with my mum and dad, you saved my life when I was depressed. You've always been there to talk to, cry to and for me to open up to about my feelings and I'll never be able to put into words just how much you mean to me.

Playing Career

Club Statistics

Club	Apps	Subs	Tries	Goals	DG	Pts
Rochdale (1998-02)	64	19	6	–	2	26
Wigan 2002-05	19	53	8	–	–	32
Castleford (2006)	18	1	4	–	1	17
Wakefield (2007-09)	18	30	2	–	–	8
Huddersfield (2009)	5	8	–	–	–	–
Widnes (2011)	1	10	–	–	–	–
Totals	125	121	20	–	3	83

Representative Honours

England A (2003)

1+3 apps, 0 points

Lancashire (2003)

1+0 apps, 0 points

England Under 21s
1+1 apps, 0 points

Northern Ford Premiership Under 21s
1+0 apps, 0 points

In Their Words ...

Watching youth rugby in the 1970s, '80s and '90s in Oldham was a real pleasure. Every school or club seemed to have youngsters, encouraged by dedicated coaches and parents, plying their skills. Defence was secondary to attack and the skill level was incredibly high. Danny was a member of that talented group, but added another quality, too – a passion to think and act outside the box that never failed to excite and amaze even the most seasoned rugby aficionado. That might be a chip or cross-field kick or a 30-yard pass, both maybe on the first tackle and maybe even in his own 20.

From a very early age he was undoubtedly a maverick and certainly aged many a coach who tried to introduce too rigid a game structure for Danny's liking! He had flair, vision and a determination to go for it and even the odd failure never quelled his enthusiasm. Many's the time he silenced vociferous opposition spectators with a piece of sublime skill that a seasoned pro would envy. On the field there was rarely a dull moment and off the field he was a larger than life character, too.

As a schoolboy at Oldham A team fixtures he sold raffle tickets for schools rugby and at the age of 13, having negotiated a generous commission deal based on past figures, achieved sales that bordered on phenomenal. There was no hiding place and he had an answer for every excuse people gave him not to buy. He even had people queuing and his 'three for 50p or five for a pound' patter worked a treat and many who bought two 50p's worth walked away chuckling and thinking they had got a bargain!

An unforgettable character.

Iain MacCorquodale, former Rochdale Hornets coach

Danny came to our club with a big reputation and also knowing he was in his brother's shadow. But it did not take long for him to prove he was a player who could stand on his own two feet. With a huge frame, great mobility, toughness and an uncanny ability to offload he was always going to have a great career in Super League.

He was an easy guy to coach with a soft nature that changed once he crossed the side-line. Danny came into a team chock full of internationals, but in the course of time became a star player in his own right.

I would like to wish Danny all the best in his future endeavours whether being in the game or elsewhere.

Stuart Raper, former Wigan coach

I first met Danny on a training course that State of Mind had set up with Jimmy Gittins and Paul Sculthorpe, to give some background to the work we were doing about mental health in clubs in December 2012.

During the day Danny talked about some of the things he had experienced and I wondered whether he would feel comfortable speaking about it in front of an audience, but he was not sure.

My knowledge of Danny came from being a rugby league supporter, who remembered a fantastic ball-playing, aggressive prop forward. Danny then agreed to talk publicly for the first time with Ste McCann and me at his speaking debut at Rochdale Mayfield on 6 February 2013 with 16 people in attendance. It was an appropriate venue because Danny had made his name there and earned a Super League contract with Wigan Warriors due to his performances for Rochdale Hornets.

The State of Mind session has been delivered many times by a number of presenters and Danny's debut was an emotional journey of his experience. It allowed him to talk about a career of 'highs and lows' and his experiences of career-ending injuries that led to a period of depressed moods and thoughts of taking his own life.

It was heart-rending, but also heart-lifting; he used his mental strength to overcome and address these dark thoughts. He became emotional which had a huge impact on the audience who were willing to tell Danny how much it had moved them. Danny saw the potential and the positive feedback was something I don't think he was expecting.

Danny has developed into an accomplished speaker who can express the powerful impact his experience has had on him and how he has used different things to help him to get back to his old self. Danny has spoken to audiences of rugby players, footballers, construction workers, school, college and university students, power workers and at conferences across the country and in Ireland.

I know how this has inspired others to get help and support and his input has saved lives more times than we may ever know. He has shown outstanding commitment as he has travelled up and down the country to deliver the mental fitness message.

We call Danny the 'Human Zoppy' (zopiclone is a sleeping medication) due to his delivery style and enthusiasm to talk about the minute details of his injuries – whether we have the time or not in any session (only joking of course).

Danny is a warm human being with a big heart and a family man who has a mischievous sense of humour. It has been an absolute honour and privilege to deliver sessions alongside him and I have been inspired by his responses to adversity and his willingness to help others.

Dr. Phil Cooper MBE, co-founder of State of Mind Sport

I am delighted to be able to provide a tribute for Danny.

As a Wigan fan, I frequently admired Danny's tenacious performances for the team, but admit to the occasional exasperation at his aggressive indiscretions, often in retaliation after having been provoked.

I especially rated his 'stand-out' ball-handling skills, which were strongly reminiscent of the flair and basketball-like skills of my all-time favourite player, Australia's Test centre Gene Miles.

I also recall Danny's raw courage in never taking a backward step.

More recently I've come to know him personally and

my regard and respect for him have expanded.

Danny has become an integral member of the State of Mind Sport team of speakers, who have received many plaudits for their insightful, humorous, moving and inspiring talks on mental fitness and resilience and the importance of seeking timely support. The courage Danny showed on the field of play he now displays in his willingness to tell the powerful story about his life-changing experiences of serious injury, enduring pain and numerous operations, which not surprisingly impacted on his emotional well-being and precipitated severe depression. In doing so, Danny meets 'head on' and pushes aside the myths and stigma of mental illness, which seriously impedes people seeking timely help and support.

As a former captain of the England RL team and recognised as a strong, tough and brave warrior, he is able to bring highly credible and persuasive messages, including that it is a strength not a weakness to seek help. This counters the macho culture endemic in northern towns, which often prevents men seeking timely help and support. Danny regularly gives targeted talks to players, schoolchildren, students and to a range of workforces.

I have received many positive comments from organisers of events and conferences following Danny's presentations, all of which mention his honesty, openness and how he has inspired the audience and given encouragement and hope to those present.

Apart from his speaking abilities, Danny has many other qualities and endearing attributes which are separate from his sporting achievements. He is naturally personable and gets on with people who respond to his warmth, wit and occasional teasing. In striking contrast to his players' role as a fearsome forward, he has demonstrated a depth of compassion and concern for others. He has been asked by the RFL to engage with former and current players who may be struggling with life pressures. His peers recognise what Danny has experienced and his own vulnerability and readily respond to him being alongside them.

I witnessed at first hand the depths of compassion he possesses when he gave his time and total attention to a bereaved mother who was acutely distressed by the loss of her son. It is clear that Dan's parents have imbued in him and his siblings strong family and caring values. He has added to these with a range of sporting values and characteristics of teamwork, discipline, determination, selflessness, responsibility, humility and passion.

I firmly believe that Danny has great potential for personal and professional development to build on his experiences, his many talents and his strong value base in order to forge a new career and a specialist niche in sport and health and well-being. His commitment to self-improvement and his passion for health and well-being are evidenced in that he has eagerly given his time and juggled with his family and other commitments to be involved in training programmes organised by PAPYRUS and the 5 Boroughs NHS Trust. This is further evidenced by Danny enrolling on a higher education counselling programme as a first step in acquiring knowledge, skills and academic qualifications, which he plans to follow through to a higher level.

In summary and by using a sporting analogy, instead of physically impacting on others and causing havoc with big hits, Danny now positively impacts on people's emotional health and the way people think and feel about themselves and others.

He has a gift to inspire optimism and hope in others.

Malcolm Rae OBE, co-founder and chairman of State of Mind Sport

It's fair to say I wouldn't be where I am today without the help of Danny, Doug and Linda. They helped me so much back in 2000 by taking me in.

I first met him when I arrived at Rochdale Hornets in November 1999. From day one he was so welcoming and you could tell he was a genuine guy who had his mates at heart. That meant we clicked straightaway. We had a couple of nights out in Oldham with the boys to get to know each other and my first one was in the Revolution Bar. Danny ordered a round of vodka shots and told me they were great, awesome flavours and I would like them.

All the boys were quick to take their shots and I, being the naive Aussie on my initiation night, was eager to quickly down mine to earn their respect! It went down pretty quickly, but within a second this burning sensation hit my throat. I started dry-retching and bringing it back up, giving me a nice double burn. My eyes were watering and I keeled over. It was the hottest thing I had ever tasted. The boys were in stitches – they had set me up with a chilli shot.

Sadly, I played only a few games for Rochdale when I was offered a payout to move on. Coach Steve Linnane drove me to Manchester Airport to drop me off to go to Australia and was good enough to walk me to the terminal to make sure I boarded my flight. He wished me well; we shook hands and parted ways.

As I went to board, I received a 'phone call to say there was an emergency and I needed to stay. I couldn't board the flight so I spoke to the air stewardess who organised for my bags to be unloaded. I spent the next week hanging out at the Sculthorpe household watching TCM with big Dougie! I had spoken to Oldham Roughyeds and had agreed I would join them. I needed a place to stay, so for the next nine months the Sculthorpe family took me in as one of their own.

For a very small boarding fee they covered my food, washed my clothes and did everything they would do for one of their own! If it was not for them doing this, I would not have had the career in the British game I did. I will always be eternally grateful for their generosity and warmth. Danny even gave up his bedroom and slept in a box-room to make me feel comfortable. It was great for me because his bedroom was massive with a kingsize bed! He slept in a tiny room on a single bed.

Danny was also my best man at my wedding and his speech is the stuff of legend. He started by downing a pint in about one-and-a-half seconds. Everyone erupted in laughter and cheered so he called over the waiter to bring him another pint. He started his speech welcoming Mr. and Mrs. McMenemy, then downed it ... and then finished his address by toasting the husband and bride with another swift one. He took three pints down within about six seconds and his speech lasted no longer than 10 minutes. On the third the whole room stood and applauded.

I should have known something would be happening when the night before we had a few beers in Halifax. The plan was to have a few quiet ones before the wedding at noon the next day. As so often happens with Danny, one thing led to another and I rolled in at 5.00am. In preparation for his speech he asked me my mother's name and being a little under the weather I announced it was Bernadette, then rolled over and went to sleep. I thought he would be going to see her in the morning so I set him up. But he actually used her name in his speech, which is all well and good, but my mother's name is Eleanor! So when Danny welcomed my parents from Australia and announced her name I just started laughing as did most of the room. He looked at me and said: 'What are you laughing at?' so I told him my mum's name is Ellie. The room had worked out what was happening by now and were laughing. Danny gave me a death stare, a stern 'Knobhead' and then continued his speech. He thought I had set him up, but I honestly had no idea he needed her name for his speech.

There was another time when we went to Blackpool for a day out – the day before Rochdale were due to face Oldham. Danny showed me around Blackpool and we finished by heading up the Tower. We were walking along in the viewing platform at the top when all of a sudden he jumped to one side and froze. I asked him what was up and he looked down. There was a section of glass floor and you could see right down to the bottom. The big fella wouldn't take another step!

The day after we beat them by a point and I kicked the winning drop goal.

It was always great playing alongside Danny and he was probably the most skilful front rower I have played with. Against him we had to lock his offload up and that was something we spoke about in our team talks. Being such a big man he was always hard to control.

Danny has the biggest heart of anyone I know and I am eternally grateful to him and his family for all their help.

I caught up with Danny and his lovely family after nine years recently and it was like we had seen each other yesterday! They are true friends forever.

Shayne McMenemy, former Rochdale Hornets teammate

It is a pleasure to be able to write just a few words about Danny during his time here at the Castleford Tigers in 2006. There are two outstanding memories of him that season. The first was his performance in a home victory over high-flyers Warrington Wolves – where Danny showed all his half-back skills that were trapped in a prop's body – as we crushed them in front of the Sky cameras. And secondly on an away trip to London where the boys got off at the services and made the schoolboy error of leaving their mobile 'phones on the seats of the bus. Anyway Danny sent all their loved ones a lovely message saying that they had 'come out of the closet and hoped they would understand'. Luckily they did.

Danny is still well thought of at the Tigers and if I was asked to paint a picture of his time here, I would have to say there isn't a canvass big enough or a colour bright enough to do it justice.

Best wishes from all at the Tigers.

Steve Gill, CEO, Castleford Tigers

A half-back in a prop's body. What immediately struck me on seeing Danny train for the first time was a ball on the side of my head. He attempted a pass I didn't think a prop could and I wasn't ready for it. He really did have incredible passing ability for a front rower.

Injuries blighted Danny's efforts in the professional game, but he can nonetheless look back on his achievements with pride.

What I would suggest should be a greater source of pride to Danny is his work with the State of Mind organisation. I've seen the impact Danny's presentations have had on audiences in the UK and Ireland in the charity's work to boost mental health and de-stigmatise mental health issues and it has a life-changing effect.

Continued success, Danny!

Brian Carney, former Wigan teammate

Danny, in my opinion, is one of the most skilful and toughest front-row forwards ever to play in the Super League. He had more skill with the ball in his hands than most half-backs and could kick the ball just as well. Scully was a great team player and was a great guy to have around.

On a number of occasions the big lad would jump in at half-back close to the line and either put a little kick through for one of the backs to chase or throw a cut-out pass for Michael Shenton to score. His skill for a big lad was impressive.

Our time at Castleford together was short, but in that period we became good mates and still to this day keep in contact with each other.

Danny Nutley, former Castleford teammate

Where can I begin when talking about Danny? My first impressions of him were of a large, committed, skilful, ball-playing forward who loved the game of rugby league.

When I came to Super League with Castleford, he was one of the senior players who I leant on for support and information on other teams. On the field he was probably the most skilful front rower I have been involved with in all my years. Those first impressions were true and with a more agile body he could have and should have been a stand-off.

I can still remember a moment from Castleford's first game back in Super League in 2006 when we played Hull at the Jungle. We were struggling to make headway and needed points. Then two minutes before half time, it was play three on the halfway line, about five metres in from touch, and Danny charged forward with everyone thinking he was carting the ball up. He had noticed their far side winger up on the end of the line and proceeded to drop the ball to his boot and kick it 40 metres across field only five metres in the air to find our winger, who then ran 50 metres to score a try in the corner.

As he kicked it, I was about to blow up in frustration; then next minute we were scoring a try. That was the type of player he was. He had great vision and could sense an opportunity when not many others could see it.

I respected Danny as a very tough team man who more often than not played under duress with a multitude of injuries. He was a real clubman who was a massively popular personality whom we all loved being around – and someone you could always rely on for an entertaining story.

On the social side of things he was a real character and

still to this day the only guy I know who can put a pint glass inside his mouth and drink from it!

Terry Matterson, former Castleford coach

Danny is a true gentleman who always shunned the limelight. He never wanted people to see the good he did. He would do what he needed to and then walk away – the mark of a true gentleman.

When we went on a pre-season tour to Orlando, he went above and beyond the call of friendship to look after me. After a training session the team went to an 'eatery', as they call if over there, and on the menu were shrimp, crab and lobster. I took one look at it and said to myself, 'I can't afford this'. Wigan paid for two meals a day, but at other times you had to pay for yourself. Kitmen don't get paid a lot of money and I couldn't afford to keep up with the lifestyle of the players. I was sitting with Danny and I said: 'What are you having?' and he replied with: 'I'm having the same as you, George.' I looked at him and said: 'The same as me?' and he said: 'Yes'. He bought me my lunch and it must have come to more than $25. Ever since I have been trying to repay him for that and look after him.

One day we came back from training and the squad were split into four vans. I was in the front with Denis Betts driving and I turned around to see Danny had gone a funny grey-green colour. I have never seen anyone go that colour in my life. I knew he injected himself through his trousers for his diabetes, but he must've forgotten or gone low. We passed a McDonald's and I shouted to Denis to pull over. I got out, ran inside and got him a Chocolate

McFlurry. After about two spoonfuls he came back to us. Ever since that day, and every match he played in, I would always carry a couple of chocolate biscuits just in case. Without the ice cream that day he would have gone into a coma.

Danny comes from a nice family and I was really proud to have been invited to his wedding alongside my wife Irene, Terry Newton and his wife, and the late Keith Mills with his wife Anne. It was a fantastic occasion and I remember him being unable to give a small speech because he kept on crying and sobbing. An emotional fella is Danny, but that is to his credit. He is a good human being.

He was very aggressive on the field, but never caused me any problems. He just got on with it and if I didn't have what he needed, he would just carry on. I remember in one game he squared up to Saints' Stuart Jones and, as they were coming off, Danny turned to him and said: 'Listen, when we go back on you can have more of the same if you like.' He was headstrong like that at times, but was such a lovely man off the field! That said, if you didn't watch him, he would dig you in the ribs as a hello. He had a big fist and a fair dig. It was a friendly tap to him, but I was careful to be aware of it.

I still see Danny quite often. If he wants a jersey or anything like that for State of Mind or other charities he is working with, I will help him out. That's not only because of what he did in America for me, but because he is a good bloke. He comes in for a chat and has about four coffees. Thing is, he always brings the coffee himself – and the biscuits! He doesn't like to sponge off anyone.

When I heard about Danny's depression I called him up and said if he ever wanted to talk to anyone, even though he had his family and friends, he could come and see me. I'm glad he did and he is a great friend.

George Unsworth, kitman, Wigan

Scully was a typical English front rower. He was a classic five-eighth in a front rower's body who had wonderful skill. He was tough, too. You could say he was one of the last of the yesteryear players. He certainly liked a beer and was a real character and in Australian terms he certainly would have fitted in great in the 1970s and '80s.

He joined us at Huddersfield from Wakefield and a change was probably what Scully needed. We were at a stage where we were playing some fair footy and he came into a side who were around the top four. His style suited what we needed – a big, tough and skilful player – and his personality was also an attraction for us. He brought all his attributes to our team and while we might have helped him a touch, he certainly helped us with his role.

We would have loved him to stay, but a big money offer from Bradford Bulls was just too much of a temptation. I know hindsight is a wonderful thing, but maybe it would have been better for Danny to stay at Huddersfield where he fit in and the way he played fit, too. When players find that happiness and a club who suit them, the extra money is probably not worth going for even though it might seem like a good thing at the time.

The thing that stuck out in his time with Huddersfield was his character and the way he played. The kid was an old-school English front rower. He was a likeable person and suited our style. His personality was great for the players we had. That type of player is all too rare these days. We don't see people like Scully now. People like characters, but we don't see them in the game as we used to. You have fond memories of that kind of bloke, but they are a dying breed in rugby league and sport in general.

Nathan Brown, former Huddersfield coach

Danny has always been a fighter and often misunderstood. As a child he was often accused of being a bully, mainly because of his size and aggression, so most of the time he played rugby league against kids two years his senior. At school he was unfairly accused of being racist, yet due to injury and illness actually spent very little time there. Later he became a target for referees, often receiving a warning before stepping on the field of play, and on numerous occasions was sent off only to be found 'not guilty' at the disciplinary.

Danny has never been one to suffer fools and was brought up to stand up for his beliefs; hence it was easy for him to fall out with certain coaches. On the field he was a throwback to the era of the ball-handling, offloading, skilful prop forwards as opposed to nowadays where yardage and line speed are paramount.

However, Danny's biggest enemy was injury. Some players are lucky, but he suffered more than most. He also had to fight a daily battle against type 1 diabetes, which slowed down any rehabilitation.

Danny's back injury at Bradford Bulls in 2009 was the start of the biggest challenge of his life and none of it was his fault. Bradford caused his injury and then took away his livelihood without a second thought. He started to feel a failure to his family and his mental health suffered. But having reached the bottom, he gathered up all his fighting instincts and started to climb back up. He has amazed us all with his strength and his willingness to channel his experiences into helping people suffering mental health problems. As a family we are all very proud of him.

Doug Sculthorpe

The best thing the RFL have done for player welfare is bringing Sporting Chance to the sport. Their work has benefited so many players, current and retired. Danny is one of those players and what is so remarkable about him is how, having struggled and come through the other side, he has now devoted his time and energy to helping others.

The work that Danny does for State of Mind is of course well-documented and his courage and commitment in talking so openly about his own story to thousands of people over the years, both in rugby league and the wider community, will have changed many lives.

Danny has also told his personal story to a meeting of the Super League CEOs to help them to understand how important the service is that Sporting Chance provides to players.

Danny always lets me know if he hears about a player (current or retired) who may be struggling a bit and helps me to make sure they get the support that's now available.

Emma Rosewarne, welfare director, Rugby Football League

I've known Danny since his early teens and even back then he was an exceptional player. He was an old fashioned prop forward with the hands of a half-back. He could pass it as well as anyone and I can't think of another prop like him, apart from Lee Crooks, in my playing days and some of the guys who played when my dad did.

I watched his career unfold – moving from Leeds to Warrington – and then when he ended up at Rochdale we met once again. I'd finished playing due to a neck injury in my early 30s and then went into coaching. Rochdale were one of my old clubs and had a place in my heart, so when Steve Deakin left, I was delighted to be named head coach. I arrived there not knowing too many of the players because I had played for ten years in the top flight and not in the Championship. But they were great to me and we had a really good blend of youth, like Danny, and experience.

Danny always wanted to play 80 minutes and even back then that was something else. At Rochdale we would spell our second rowers every 20 minutes and it seemed to work for us. Danny was full of life and never wanted to come off the field. He wanted to be involved in every play. He had enthusiasm for the game and great knowledge of it, too, for such a young lad.

I know he had setbacks with injury, but he was resilient, too. One time he went over on his ankle in training a few days before a big game against Swinton. His ankle was swollen up and he couldn't train on the Saturday. But come Sunday he'd somehow got himself right and had one of his typical games for us. We beat Mike Gregory's Swinton and he was superb.

I saw the emotional side of him, too, but I never had an issue with him all the time I was coaching. He was opinionated and quite vocal at times, but not once did I have to say anything to him. He never said anything detrimental to the team, coaching staff or anyone at the club. That is a good attitude to have and he was exemplary.

He was great to have in that team and we went well. We got beaten by Oldham in the semifinal that year and then he went on to Wigan. I went from Rochdale to Wigan, too, in my playing career so it was a familiar path.

I always knew he would do well. He had the talent and application and my only concern was if the injuries would be an issue. He was always destined to do better things and, given the difficulties he's been through in recent years, I guess you sometimes have to take a backward step to move forward.

He was a great character off the field, too. He could drink a quick pint for sure! I rarely socialised with the players when I was coach, but I did go on his stag do in later years. That was a special night in Wetherby and Leeds for sure!

Martin Hall, former Rochdale Hornets coach

When we started Royton Tigers in 1986, we had some early coaching sessions with about 50 kids aged under 11 trying rugby league for the first time. Among those first kids were two brothers, Paul and Danny Sculthorpe. Two weeks later Paul played and scored in his first match for the Under 11 team and another 14 days later Danny did the same for the Under 9s in his first game. Although he was only seven-years-old, Danny was soon to become the team leader and the player everyone looked up to. His presence was so powerful, something he continued throughout his playing career.

Danny wanted to be different; he would throw long passes and completely outfox other teams and even at seven-years-of-age he always seemed destined for greatness.

As a coach he was a joy to have at training because he was always keen to learn and willing to try new things. Danny loved tackling and encouraged his teammates, who were less skilled than him, to perform better. And when he lost – something he hated – it made him more determined to improve.

Later I was present when Danny and Paul faced each other in the Challenge Cup final. What a great feeling that was as I reflected on those early coaching sessions we had together!

Well done, Danny, I'm proud to have been at the start of your career.

Steve Bithell, founder, Royton Tigers

For years the Australian rugby league fraternity have often referred to ball-handling forwards as an English-type forward. And they found it difficult to deal with the big, strong, powerful forwards who could also pass the football with ease.

Having grown up in Lancashire and witnessed many great ball-playing English forwards, it was no surprise to me that many of the big men had those skills and we almost took it for granted. Players such as Brian McTigue and Vince Karalius were tough men, but they also had football brains. Alex Murphy scored many tries from passes from Vince Karalius.

It's fair to say that such skilful forwards are not necessarily a feature in our modern game. It was a delight, therefore, when we saw Danny Sculthorpe play and display fabulous ball-handling skills. He was of course also a big, strong, fearless prop forward, so we were looking at the complete package.

Players as big as Danny with such exceptional handling skills don't come along very often and I was delighted when we were able to sign him for Wigan.

Sadly for Danny, he joined us at a time when we were struggling. His natural attacking skills were somewhat wasted although his contribution, nevertheless, was terrific.

It has been sad to observe that Danny's health has made life difficult for him and we all hope that he soldiers on in the way that prop forwards always seem to do so bravely.

Maurice Lindsay, former chairman, Wigan Warriors

Danny was a bit of an idiot growing up, but really fun to be around. Paul and Danny would fight constantly and I was always the one who had to split them up. In the end it always ended up being me and Danny against Paul, trying to fill him in. After that I would have to fix the furniture they'd smashed up and often I would be looking for a knife because I couldn't find a screwdriver to mend the TV cabinet or a hat stand that had become part of the collateral damage. There was also a time Paul punched a hole through the bathroom door because he was trying to hit Danny and missed. They were intensely competitive and neither of them wanted to back down. As a result it was great fun growing up with them.

I played football at Failsworth Tigers and never really got into rugby until I was 12-years-old. They were both playing by then and Dad kept on mithering for me to play a decent sport. I eventually gave in and loved it. It was good watching them both grow up and I ended up playing with Danny at Rochdale. We were a real duo because we were handy on the field and liked to give it out a bit. I played six games in the first team with him and a few in the reserves. One that sticks out is when we played with my mate, Paul Geener. He was handy, too, and the three of us went around in a pack trying to batter everyone!

Danny is the best player I have played with and skill-wise he was superb. I have never known a player with better hands than he has. He was real quality and I always knew he would play at the top. After being at Leeds and Warrington, he took a step back going to Rochdale, but it was the best thing he ever did. He was too good for that level and I knew a big club would snap him up because he was awesome there.

Danny was a mentally tough player and a lot of people would have packed in if they'd suffered the injuries he had. He kept on going through adversity and Paul was the same, too. That came from our Dad. He always told us never to give up and if anyone tried to get one over you, you had to give it them back. He told us never to back down and they have both embraced that.

I remember when we worked together at a sheet metal shop. He would come in on a Monday at 8.00am after getting in from a night out only three hours earlier. He would go to sleep in the toilets; you could tell he'd been there because, when you went in to use the loo, there would be arse cheek marks in the dust behind the door! He'd also insist on doing the chippy runs at dinner time a good two hours early so he could fall asleep in his car. Like I say, Danny was proper daft at times, but real fun!

I'm immensely proud of what he has achieved considering what he has been through. He is a role model for people with diabetes, too, and I know that because I am also type 1.

He is someone to look up to without a doubt.

Lee Sculthorpe

I first played with Danny at Waterhead which was originally Oldham Juniors, then alongside him in the Oldham town teams, Lancashire and when he captained England at Under 16s. He was very strong and powerful and had an unbelievable skillset for a front rower. He possessed a good passing and kicking game and was almost a throwback to a Lee Crooks or David Hobbs in his style. He was great to be around and we would spend a lot of time together on the park at Waterhead practising our goal-kicking skills because he was good at that, too.

I also had the pleasure of facing him a number of times at High School. He was aggressive and dominant in the teams he played for. He could carry the ball hard at you and had an unbelievable offload. You'd work him down to the floor and think you had him nailed when the ball would pop out into the hands of a teammate.

Growing up in Oldham, there were some good players around, but Danny was always one of those who stood out. And when he joined the professional ranks, he still stood out even though he had other talented players around him. That compulsive offload game he had in his junior days shone through and he was just as tough and uncompromising.

He was blighted with injuries towards the back end of his career, but I do think if he had avoided those, he would definitely have been right up there with some of the finest front rowers this country has ever seen.

Although he has been through a lot, I still see Danny exactly in the same way as I did when I was 11-years-old. He was always an inspirational character and a good mate and that hasn't changed. When I look at what happened after his career, how he handled it and the work he does now, that is inspirational too. I think for him to be out there helping people by passing on his story, knowledge and experience is superb.

The great thing about our sport is that we have the likes of Danny who are prepared to give of themselves for the betterment of others. He has done that and that is the mark of a special man.

I'll end with a story. When we both signed for Leeds, we became very close and I remember those days as a really good time in my youth. When we came away from the Rhinos early on, we were given a bag of kit and Danny wore his into Oldham Town Centre. He must have had his tracksuit on for no longer than three hours when a pigeon crapped on his shoulder. It's something that has always tickled me!

Kevin Sinfield MBE, former school teammate

Growing up, Danny and I always seemed to be fighting. We would be messing about with a ball and wrestling like rough lads do, which would soon descend into a full-on fight. I don't know if it was because we were fairly close in age, but we never got on. One thing would lead to another, Danny and I would start fighting and then Lee would come in and back him up. I always seemed to get the rough end of it from them both. We would smash the house up by falling into TV cabinets and knocking off ornaments when we were scrapping and then join forces to fix things up before Mum and Dad came back in.

We just didn't get on at all and that seemed to carry on until Jon Roper's wedding. Late on in the night he was obviously upset and said he couldn't believe we had always fallen out when it was clear we cared so much about each other. Danny has always been an emotional person and this started a new chapter in the relationship between us. We have been very close ever since.

Oddly, while the three of us would get stuck into each other when we were young, if anyone else tried anything on one of us, the other two would come to his defence. I remember one time in Royton there were three brothers who were troublemakers. We called them the Duffel Coat Gang and one day they started on one of us. All three of them got leathered as a result because we backed each other up; we had a strong family bond and that continues now.

When we first started playing rugby, it was clear Danny had talent. He got a bit of stick when he was younger because he was a big kid, but he had some good coaches, including Phil McLean who got him to work on his skills. Phil didn't want him to get through just by being the biggest kid because, when you get older, there comes a time when you aren't the biggest any more.

He took those skills into the professional game. He was

physical and aggressive as a youngster, but also one of the most skilful players I have ever seen. It was unbelievable how he could pass and kick a ball and he showed that throughout his career. That is why he played at the top and for Great Britain Under 21s, England and in a Challenge Cup final to name but a few highlights.

He had some bad luck with injuries and not just when he got older. He dislocated his knee and was diagnosed with diabetes in his teens and struggled with that early on. He eventually controlled it by finding the right lifestyle. I know that must have been hard for him, just as it is for young kids now who are diagnosed with the condition and don't know if they can do all the things they want to. Danny is a big inspiration to a lot of people with diabetes in showing how you can get on in sport and life when you have the condition.

When you played against Danny, you knew it was going to be physical. He always tried to give it to me more than anyone else and to be honest I tried to give it back as well, but he was just too big. One time we played Wigan and David Vaealiki gave me a crack. My natural response, as always, was to give one back. I was underneath in the tackle with the ball in one hand, but managed to throw one with my other hand. But Danny instantly dived on me and held my arms down while Vaealiki hit me with a couple. Brotherly love that. He was right, though – on the field you are just another player.

I also remember a time I was playing for Saints at Wigan. Danny came off the bench and with his first touch came straight through our defence and offloaded for Adrian Lam to go under the sticks. Behind the posts we decided that Sean Long should kick the ball straight into Danny's arms and Jason Hooper and I would try to stick him into the back of the South Stand. Longy kicked off and Hoops and I flew in ... but he bumped straight through us both and put Brett Dallas away for a length-of-the-field try. He made us look foolish, but that was his ability. He was an old-school prop, but I think that type of player should be encouraged in the modern game.

It's sad I didn't get the chance to play with Danny professionally. We got close when we were both selected for Lancashire, but I pulled out the week before with a hamstring problem. He was also linked with Saints a few times, but we never got the chance to be on the same side.

When I see what he has done since his playing days it makes me very proud, but then I always was proud of him anyway. He has always been an emotional person who can't say stuff in front of his family without his lip going. I am very much the same, too, when it comes to family members and people I care for. I think that was the issue when he was going through the difficult times, the feeling he was letting everyone down. It was hard to watch, but all we could do was to be there for him and be positive and encouraging. He had to be the one to instigate it and be willing to open up. He was brave enough to do that and that sets a massive example for others in his work with State of Mind. If a big 17-stone rugby player who is supposed to be bullet-proof can speak about mental issues, then anyone can. It isn't a weakness to talk about depression; it shows his strength in having the courage to seek help. That is powerful – and Danny is a passionate advocate of the work of State of Mind.

Danny is a great brother and friend and Nat and their kids are superb, too. We are really close and see each other all the time. That family bond comes through our parents and you couldn't ask for a better mum and dad. They instilled in all three of us that family bond and we are as close as ever.

Paul Sculthorpe MBE

Helpful Websites

State of Mind
www.rugbyleague.stateofmindsport.org

Samaritans
www.samaritans.org
Telephone: 116 123 (24 hours daily)

CALM
CALM, the campaign against living miserably, is a charity set up in response to the high suicide rate among young men.
www.thecalmzone.net
Telephone: 0800 58 58 58 (5pm until midnight)

Mind
www.mind.org.uk
Telephone: 0300 123 3393 (9am to 6pm Mon to Fri)

PAPYRUS
Founded in 1997 by Jean Kerr, a mother from Lancashire. She and a small group of parents who had each lost a child to suicide were convinced that that many young suicides

are preventable.
www.papyrus-uk.org
Telephone: 0800 068 41 41 (10am to 10pm Mon to Fri, 2pm to 10pm weekends)

Survivors of Bereavement by Suicide
This organisation exists to meet the needs and break the isolation of those bereaved by the suicide of a close relative or friend.
www.uk-sobs.org.uk
Telephone: 0300 111 5065 (9am to 9pm daily)

Connecting With People
Open Minds Alliance CIC was formally established in 2010. The organisation emerged from a collaboration between Dr. Alys Cole-King, liaison psychiatrist and specialist in suicide prevention, and Gavin Peake-Jones, a specialist in implementing transformation in organisations.
www.connectingwithpeople.org/ucancope

Self-Help
A user-led mental health charity based in the North of England. They are there to provide the support, advice, tools and techniques you need to help you to take control of your life.
www.selfhelpservices.org.uk
Telephone: 0300 003 7029 (8pm to 6am)